ANCIENT INDIAN HISTORY

RAJEEV AGARWAL

New Delhi • London

BLUEROSE PUBLISHERS
India | U.K.

Copyright © Rajeev Agarwal 2025

All rights reserved by author. No part of this publication may be reproduced, stored in a retrieval system or transmitted in any form or by any means, electronic, mechanical, photocopying, recording or otherwise, without the prior permission of the author. Although every precaution has been taken to verify the accuracy of the information contained herein, the publisher assumes no responsibility for any errors or omissions. No liability is assumed for damages that may result from the use of information contained within.

BlueRose Publishers takes no responsibility for any damages, losses, or liabilities that may arise from the use or misuse of the information, products, or services provided in this publication.

For permissions requests or inquiries regarding this publication, please contact:

BLUEROSE PUBLISHERS
www.BlueRoseONE.com
info@bluerosepublishers.com
+91 8882 898 898
+4407342408967

ISBN: 978-93-6783-391-9

Cover design: Yash Singhal
Typesetting: Namrata Saini

First Edition: January 2025

DISCLAIMER

Ancient Indian History is a comprehensive exploration of India's rich past, based on my research and interpretation of key events and civilizations. The journey through time presented in this book is not meant to be an exhaustive historical account but an immersive experience into the profound contributions of ancient Indian civilizations.

All images included in this book are credited to their respective owners, with most sourced from Wikipedia. I acknowledge and respect the intellectual property of the original creators. If any attributions are missing or incorrect, I welcome the rightful owners to contact me so that necessary updates can be made in future editions.

I appreciate your interest in this fascinating subject and hope this work serves to deepen your understanding of ancient India's lasting impact on the world.

CONTENTS

Chapter 1: The Indus Valley Civilization..................1

Introduction..1
Major Cities and Towns...8
The Phases of Harappan Culture 12
Early Indus/ Harappan Period 3500 BCE to
2500 BCE..13
Mature Indus Period 2500 BCE To 1800 BCE.......16
Development of Trade And Infrastructure................21
Late Harappan Period 1800 BCE To 1400 BCE.....25
Mesopotamia—Major Trade Partner........................25
Political and Social Structure......................................30
Social Structure And Harappan Mythology..............33
Decline and Collapse of The Civilization 38
Change in Weather Conditions 39
Cessation of trade...42
Change in the course of the Indus River 43
Foreign Invasion 43
Integration into The Aryan Culture 45

Chapter 2: The Vedic Period....................................47

Introduction..47
Seven Rivers (Sapta Sindhu)......................................51
Vedic Literature..56
Rishis And Their Disclosures: 65
Oral Transmission: 65
Preservation And Compilation: 65

Chapter 3: The Mahajanapadas 71

Chapter 4: Buddhism 79

Introduction 79
The Four Noble Truths In Brief 83
The Eightfold Path In Brief 84
Buddhist Councils: 89
Hinayana And Mahayana: 91
Contribution of Buddhism to Indian Culture: 91
Decline of Buddhism: 93

Chapter 5: Jainism 97

Teachings of Mahaveer Swami Ji and
Principles of Jainism 100
Contributions of Jainism to Indian Culture 104
Decline of Jainism In India: 105

Chapter 6: Alexander Conquest of India 109

Chapter 7: Vishnugupt (Chanakya) and Dhana Nand 112

Chapter 8: Seleucus 1 Nikator 120

Chapter 9: The Mauryan Empire 123

Chandragupta Maurya (320 BCE to 298 BCE) 123
Bindusara (320 BCE—273 BCE) 129
Ashoka the Great (268 BCE—232 BCE) 132
Battle of Kalinga (261 B.C.) 134
Sources of Mauryan History 136
The Arthashastra 136
The Book "Indica" of Megasthenes 137
Mudra Rakshasa of Visakadutta 138
Ashokas Rock Edicts 139

Fourteen Major Rock Edicts.................................. 139
Seven Pillar Edicts.. 139
Two Minor Rock Edicts... 140
Four Minor Pillar Edicts.. 140
Cave Inscriptions... 140
The Administration of The Maurya Empire.......... 141
Central Government 141
Military Administration... 143
Espionage System 144
Judicial Administration.. 145
Provincial Administration...................................... 146
Local Administration 147
The Dhamma or Dharma of Ashoka 147
Causes for The Downfall of The Mauryan
Empire.. 149

Chapter 10: The Classical Period Part 1.............. 151

The Shungas... 152
The Indo-Greeks.. 156
The Satvahanas... 158
Architecture in the Satvahana Phase..................... 161
The Shakas... 162
The Parthians... 164
The Kushans... 165
The Indo-Sassanians 168
The Classical Period Part 2 171
The Gupta Empire... 171
The Kamarupas.. 174
The Southern Kingdoms 176
Vardhan Dynasty 182

Chapter 11: Sangam Literature............................ 192

CHAPTER 1
THE INDUS VALLEY CIVILIZATION

INTRODUCTION

The Indus Valley civilization was structured in present-day Pakistan and northwestern India around 3500 BCE. This makes it one of the oldest social and cultural development in the world, which survived until about 1300 BCE, approximating about two thousand years. It was one of the largest urban and culturally developed states belonging to the very distant past and is no longer in existence. At its pinnacle, it incorporated more than six million inhabitants and occupied an area far bigger than Egypt of those times and Mesopotamia. Interestingly, the most surprising fact about this culture is that, until about a hundred years ago, no one even believed it existed to be true and had no certain proof.

The initial humans lived in the Indus River Valley and surfaced around 8000 BCE. They were a group of people who had an occurring undivided liking for wandering, hunting, and searching for food. These people lived in medium-sized groups, and their dwellings comprised small and easily movable homes. Around 6500 BCE, some of these people began to use simple handmade devices, which helped them to build permanent establishments and practice farming. They stopped being wanderers, stationed themselves in one place, and became somewhat inactive.

The dilapidated and disintegrated parts of the city were first rediscovered between 1820 and 1826 in the Sahiwal District of Pakistan, pretty close to the Indian border. Historians and surveyors' detection of Harappa challenged the beliefs of most Western historians and archaeologists, who had a totally different view on early human settlement.

Around 1853, workers were building the first ever railway in India, a stretch between Lahore and other major cities of northwest India, which later became the Punjab Railway. The British engineers who observed and directly supervised the execution task of the primordial workers, who were digging and underpinning the Multan-Lahore section of the track, discovered thousands of mud bricks sunken in the earth. The British engineers were happy and showed great pleasure as bricks were in short supply. There was a shortage of material in that particular area, and these bricks were perfectly suitable to give stability to the track bed.

The engineers though not fully qualified for archaeological assessment were trying to figure out where these bricks, which could be easily perceived to be ancient, had initially come from. While laying out another section of the rail track, these heavy bricks again appeared. Apart from being an excellent source of construction material., these bricks designated and unearthed the possibility of unknown physical destruction or disintegration in the area. Till then, the only known older Indian civilization was one formed by Aryans, who came from central Asia. But the establishment of Aryans in the northwest of India was ultimately ruled out because they settled mainly in the eastern side, namely the Ganges valley, which is geographically very far.

The city was subject to an intensive archaeological expedition in 1920 and 1921, a project led by Shri Daya Ram Sahni. He is known for his notable work on the excavation of the Indus valley site., upon which he was appointed as the director general of the Archeological Survey of India. He was also awarded the title of "RAI BAHADUR" by the governor of Punjab in the year 1920. From Sahni and other archaeologists who came in after him, excavators and historiographers learned that the Indus Valley cities of Harappa and other modern cities along the Indus and Sarasvati were exceptionally well constructed and arranged. The layout of the cities was very neatly designed and made. One of the greatest works and structures was THE GREAT BATH., found in one of the exemplary cities of Mohenjo Daro. Along with every structure in the entire city, it was linked via underground ducts to a smart drainage system that was comparable and contended to the modern systems. They had all the natural resources at their disposal., and were able to produce abundant food supplies., trade, and excellent means of peace and harmonious community living. The people had a simple life and were God-fearing. Agriculture and farming methods were conventional., and cattle was a major parameter for measuring wealth.

The term *Harappan* is applicable to the Indus civilization after its city Harappa, which was one of the first to be excavated early in the then province of Punjab, British India. The discovery of Harappa and, later on

Mohenjo-Daro was the zenith of excavation that had been undertaken after establishing the Archaeological Survey of India in 1861. There were earlier and later civilizations called Early Harappan and Late Harappan. The early Harappan cultures were inhabited and settled from the neolithic era, the most prominent one being Mehrgarh in Balochistan., present-day Pakistan. This will be discussed in detail later on in this book. Harappan civilization is also called *Mature Harappan* to distinguish it from the earlier cultures.

The Indus Valley Civilization is in a class by itself among the other ancient civilizations for many reasons. First and most notably, it has the privilege of occupying a very large area comprising present-day India and Pakistan. Moreover, its uniqueness is that it did so without any military intervention and without taking control of any other cultures whatsoever. We have many other civilizations which were made and molded thru military power. Almost every other equivalent civilization was established through conquest and warfare.

After the civilization declined, nothing much was left other than old bricks buried in the ground. As their buildings and architectural structures collapsed, these people were forgotten and were never thought of. Historians have opined that the Indus people did not indulge in any sort of warfare as most other ancient civilizations. It was unlikely that they tried to conquer other cultures, and there were no indications of any military intervention or weapons in archaeological excavations of Indus Valley Civilization sites.

The Indus River Valley lies majorly in today's Pakistan. From this fertile area, the Indian civilization arose. What is worth noticing is the fact that the majority of the settlements of this old civilization have not been situated on the banks of the Indus but on the wrinkled and withered course of the Sarasvati River. Indeed, 80% of the metropolitan settlements of that period were found along the course of the Sarasvati River. The Sarasvati then, at that point, was the main core of the Harappan civilization. The Sarasvati is also mentioned in the Rig Veda. It was called Sindhu Mata—the mother of the Indus.

The Indian independence in 1947 led to the creation of two separate and autonomous countries: India and Pakistan. A significant portion of the Indus Valley Civilization was in the Punjab, which became a part of Pakistan. However, as more and more territories were discovered, it came to light that the area controlled by the Harappans was much larger than previously understood. New sites have been found, not just in other parts of Pakistan and India but as far north as present-day Afghanistan. To the present day, more than 1,000 archaeological sites that appear to have belonged to this society have been uncovered, and more are being discovered almost every year. It is generally accepted that the Indus Valley was one of the three Ancient civilizations of the east, considered to be the cradles of civilization. However, the other two (Egypt and Mesopotamia) left written records, which means we know a great deal about those people. The Indus people left few written records, and the inscriptions which have been found on seals and other artifacts have not yet been deciphered. This means that we know comparatively little about this civilization, although it may have been the largest of all.

To the early people, the Indus River Valley and the Saraswati River provided the reservoir they needed to build cities to combine and integrate their wealth. As early as 3400 BCE, the river valley blossomed with civil structures, agriculture, and trade that stretched from modern Afghanistan into northern India. As many as six million people may have lived here during the peak of civilization. The Indus Valley's main feature was the river stretching southwest across Pakistan until merging into the Arabian Sea. It was a powerful and highly attractive stretch of fertile, water-adjacent land for the local inhabitants and immigrants even thousands of years before large cities appeared. The people began to think about the valley as their permanent settlement, which promised a bright future not only for them but for generations to come. They learned about agriculture, certain crop cultivation, and brick-making for construction purposes.

The Sarasvati people successfully evolved regular trade routes, methods of powerful shipbuilding, and planning of sea routes so that they might visit the states and homelands of the east and west, including Mesopotamia and Egypt. There, they brought their own precious metals, wood, ivory, and cotton and purchased other articles to get back to India. Archaeologists have found many of these items in unusual Indus Valley locations, which are not indigenous, establishing a connection or link between neighboring communities and society.

Many excavation sites, such as Rupar and Kalibangan, did not divulge and disclose products of specialized artifacts that belonged to any ancient culture. There have been copper blades and swords exhumed at these places, as well as collections of clay balls concocted to have been used in defense of the people. Any artwork depicting any sort of warfare is very less, but it cannot be totally ruled out that the early natives of the Indus Valley were absolutely without violence and never had any sort of serious disagreement amongst themselves.

The general public living in the early Indus period would have mainly been farmers and agriculturists. As time went on, they developed and looked out for other kinds of careers. Trading and craftsmanship developed as full-time jobs for many. Archaeologists were able to uncover only Pottery, as other goods and articles might have deteriorated. The possibility of cloth making from cotton is highly assumed, but it failed to find traces. Some artistic items recovered include beads, hard shells, and stone pieces, drilled, tied, and bound together by strings, presumed to be jewelry. The most common handmade things and items were likely within reach of the common people. The more scarce the items, the more chance that they would have been owned by the wealthy. But in a way, the products were not tough and durable.

The cities of this bygone civilization were very incompatible. Dissimilar to every other ancient city, they did not develop as elements of an organized economy over time in an unmethodical way. Instead, they were cautiously formulated and had distinctive attributes of elegant, refined personal hygiene and waste management systems around 3,500 years before such systems became known to everyone elsewhere in the world. They initiated advanced studies and research in metals and medicine. This civilization is the most remarkable and worthy of attention. It is authoritative, prominent, and most prestigious among all primordial civilizations belonging to the distant past., yet it is one about which we still know proportionately very little. Even today, understanding of this culture is making progress and unfolding with new learning. It firmly makes us believe that there is still a great deal to be found about the bewildering Indus people.

Experts in history do not know what the set of formal legal institutions that constituted a state or government was like. However, considering the implementation of standards in everything they did, from city framework patterns to drainage systems, it is likely that they had some kind of regulatory authority. Various theories range from the Harappans having many crowned heads instead of one central head or maybe they had landlords who ruled the common people.

MAJOR CITIES AND TOWNS

Let us study the major cities of the Indus valley civilization in detail. The Indus valley civilization was spread out in modern-day Pakistan and northwestern parts of India. Some of the largest cities were Mohenjo-Daro and Harappa, both located in modern-day Pakistan. At different times, each of these cities would be the capital of the Indus Valley civilization. Dholavira was another major urban center and was located in modern-day India. Dholavira is also the second-largest Indus Valley city that historians know about. More is known about Mohenjo-Daro and Harappa than Dholavira. However, historians and archaeologists are still studying the Indus Valley area and learning more about it all the time. Mohenjo-Daro, also called Mohenjodaro and Moenjodaro, is one of the most famous Indus Valley cities. This city was built along the Indus River in modern-day southern Pakistan. Because of various environmental changes over the last few millennia, the site is about three kilometers away from the river. In total, the city had an area of about 750 acres. At its peak, it could have held up to forty thousand people comfortably, making it one of the largest and most populous cities. Mohenjo-daro's name roughly translates to "Mound of the Dead." This name was given by archaeologists who found the city. This name could have come from the fact that the city's founders built a synthetic base for one area of the town. However, historians do not know exactly what the city's original name was. This mound was made of mud bricks and used mud as a type of mortar. Later, buildings were erected on top of the mound.

Impressively, the bricks had a uniform shape and weight. This showed that the Indus Valley had a complex civil engineering forte. Many of these buildings were large structures, which could have included both homes and government-like buildings. These buildings were also made of mud bricks. There may have been some wood or hay used in the construction as well, but these would have decayed so that they would have been unnoticed by the archaeologists today. Another fantastic feature of Mohenjo-Daro was its rectangular grid system and paved roads. These roads were also made out of mud bricks. The city had a unique sewer system, complete with drainage systems. Oddly enough, architects have not been able to find any elaborate palaces, religious buildings, or government buildings in Mohenjo-Daro. There were smaller administrative buildings in the town and even buildings that were apartments. Other than these, most buildings would have been average houses and marketplaces. Mohenjo-Daro was one of the most progressive cities in the ancient world. Historians aren't sure when the city's inhabitants began to move away from Mohenjo-Daro. There are some pieces of evidence indicating that floods from the Indus River may have done damage to the town. However, other historians think the Saraswati River dried up or changed its course as years passed, causing a drought. It is also possible that both of these events happened at different times. Either way, the city collapsed near the end of the Indus Valley civilization around 1300 BCE. For centuries after civilization ended, the city was lost to time.

Harappa was one of the first Indus Valley civilization sites to be discovered by archaeologists somewhere in 1920. Because of this, the Indus Valley civilization is also called the Harappan civilization. Harappa is likely the oldest urban center in the Indus Valley and was first settled around 3500 BCE. Harappa was built along the Ravi River. This was the most outstanding advantage Harappa as a city had, and it put Harappa right in a flood plain, which made the land fertile and great for farming. It was also in an ideal location to promote trade with other civilizations that existed and occurred during the same time. This enabled the people in Harappa to interact with different cultures. This can also be said due to artifacts from other civilizations that have been found in Harappa. Harappa was one of the capitals of the Indus Valley civilization. The city was about half the size of Mohenjo-daro near its beginning, only covering about four hundred acres. Still, about twenty to thirty thousand people could live there comfortably. Harappa hit its peak around 2200 BCE, with an estimated population of nearly eighty thousand inhabitants. However, these numbers are estimated and are debatable by historians. By looking at various artifacts, archaeologists guess that Harappa grew from a village to an urban center sometime during the Harappan phase. The archaeologists determined this based on writings and other artifacts from the period.

However, while historians have found writings from the Indus Valley civilization, they cannot yet read them. During the Ravi phase, people started to move into Harappa. These people likely came from areas relatively close to Harappa rather than traveling far distances. The first people who lived here held a variety of careers and had many different skills. Archaeologists have explored all kinds of art and crafts in the area, from beads of various shapes and sizes and stones to large sculptures. These items were made out of all types of materials and multiple stones. It was likely that some trade was going on in the area at that time. Archaeologists know this because arts and crafts made of beads and stones in the Indus Valley have also been found at ancient Mesopotamian sites. It is not likely that these beads could have got there without trade. Even brick-making by the people of Harappa developed in that phase. While there had been some buildings before this time, it was during this phase that the mud bricks became standardized, meaning they had standardized shapes and sizes. These bricks lined most of the buildings and streets in Harappa. It was also during this period that Harappans began to build brick walls around the city. The buildings and even cemetery plots had different shapes, sizes, and styles. Accordingly, Archaeologists determined the other social classes from the time period. This might suggest that the Indus people had an economic system in place.

The Indus Valley civilization continued to stretch and thicken during the Harappan phase. The people had spread out, gaining access and control of more land areas. It is more likely that small land areas were ruled by the rich, like the merchants and landowners. During this time, artisans improved their crafts. They started making shiny ceramics and tools of various shapes and sizes that could be used.

During the Late Harappan Transitional and Late Harappan periods, people moved away from the cities and into more rural areas. This started to break up the cities, with the large urban centers getting smaller and other small cities (suburbs) cropping up around them. However, this made the cities weak and more prone to infiltration. All of this, along with climate change, disease, and the loss of trade partners, led to the decline of the Harappan civilization., which will be discussed later in this book.

THE PHASES OF HARAPPAN CULTURE

The exact timeline of the Indus Valley Civilization is not known, and different historians have different views regarding the stages of development of the civilization. For further understanding, the Indus valley civilization can be studied in three periods. The Early Harappan Phase (3500 to 2500 BCE), the Mature Harappan Phase (2500 to 1800 BCE), and the Late Harappan Phase (1800 to 1300 BCE). Archaeologists determined the beginning and end dates of these stages based on what types of crafts and technologies were found.

EARLY INDUS/ HARAPPAN PERIOD 3500 BCE TO 2500 BCE

The early Harappan period ranges between 3500 BCE to 2600 BCE. The earlier people to settle in the Indus valley were the ones who settled in an area that was very close to the Ravi river. Hence the early Indus Phase is also called the Ravi Phase. The early years of the Indus Valley civilization, known as the early span and Ravi period, determined how the Harappan culture would grow and evolve over its two-thousand-year history. The early people traveled westward, originating from the mountainous region between or around modern-day Pakistan, Afghanistan, and Iran. Settlers may have even come from as far as ancient Mesopotamia, which was mostly located in the modern-day Middle East. The first settlers were likely farmers and other common people. Wealthier groups of people followed in their footsteps later. Once more groups entered the cities, a social hierarchy began to form.

Whatever formed and shaped this civilization was greatly influenced by its location. The prime reason for the success of this civilization was its geographical positioning, soil fertility, and the rivers and seas, which had a great impact on day-to-day life. The first villages began to show up in the Indus River Valley around 3300 BCE. They formed around the Ravi River and spread out from there. During this period, the city of Harappa was built, and the Indus Valley civilization started to standardize building methods. Historians had very solid reasons to believe that the main city of Harappa began to prosper because it was located on an important junction of many prominent trade routes which linked the upper plains with the southern plains. Another reason for them to believe this city being a large trade hub was that upon excavation, Harappa unearthed many man-made articles of cultural and historical interests, which were from other areas. These artifacts might have been brought from distant lands and places for trading.

In its earliest stages, almost all buildings were constructed from mud bricks made in brick molds. Carvings in bricks and other stones used for construction purposes with designs were not known. Other crafts also grew rapidly in the early stages of Harappa. Many figures and toys of terracotta (baked clay) resembling human beings and animals have been found by archaeologists. The early Harappan people would also have been known to produce cloth, as pieces of equipment relating to textile products, such as weaving tools and patterns of concentric circles of clay spindles were found. All the above findings suggest that the early Harappan society was complex and multi-layered, with individuals comprising different works and occupations such as farming, skilled craftsmen, traders, and merchants. Initially, the city was spread over a small area and had two or three small settlements in the north and south.

By 2600 BCE, the city expanded rapidly and the people had constructed boundary walls of mud and bricks to protect themselves from wild animals. Large gateways were made to enter and exit the city. Town planning and designing also became a little more advanced in this period. Most buildings within the city were constructed on raised levels made of bricks that elevated them above the ground. They also had sophisticated and well-designed personal hygiene and drainage system. It was more advanced and classy than the cities of Mesopotamia and Egypt. Many houses had their own personal wells, which had clean drinkable water. They had baths and flush toilets, which emptied into the sewage system below. Large clay pots and soil tanks made of bricks were used as septic tanks. These tanks had manhole covers to enable timely cleaning and maintenance.

Such complex, smart sanitation and excellent waste-discarding systems have not been found in any other primordial culture. Such sanitation systems were not even known in Europe and other developed parts of the world till 1500 CE. Town planning was also very appropriate, and it had areas designated for residences, markets, commercial storage, etc. The city had large and small settlements on river banks widely spread all across present-day western Punjab and Sindh. Administrators had developed excellent surface trade routes linking Harappa to other major cities, such as Mohenjo Daro and Dholavira.

MATURE INDUS PERIOD
2500 BCE TO 1800 BCE

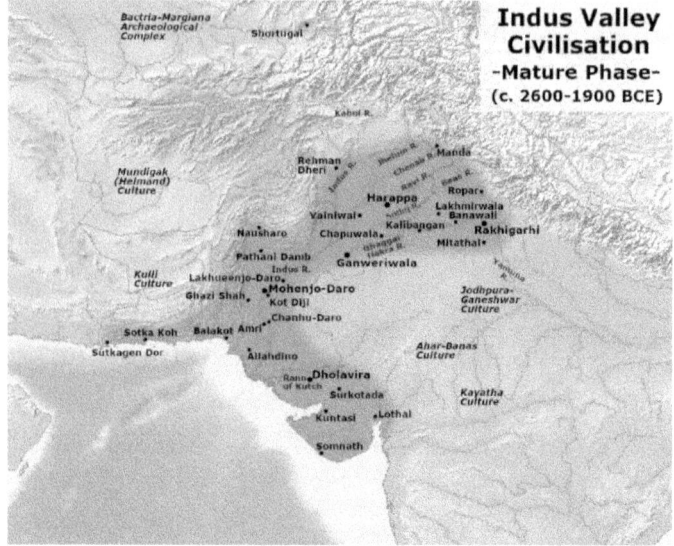

Indus Valley Mature Phase

The later stage of the Indus Valley civilization is known as the mature period consolidation age, which ranges from 2500 BCE to 1800 BCE. During this period, cities expanded and became more systematic. Mesh patterns, writing, and the directives made and maintained by the authority of supplies all came into existence. Little availability of facts and information showed that social, money-spinning, and commercial classes of society started to manifest, which also influenced how cities were arranged and assembled. This span could have been used to qualify the statement of the opinion that it w the beginning of city-states in the Indus Valley. All in all, this could have been the most fruitful and fertile period for the Indus Valley civilization. In fact, it can also be termed as the rearmost period of civilization before its commencement to downfall.

The inhabitants of the valley had begun to take an active interest in agriculture around 3600 BCE. At first, they gave prominence to farming wheat, beans, and condiments. As the years went on and as the weather changed, they stretched their crop-growing endeavors to more varieties of grains. Farming is the root and emergence of any great civilization, which supports the fact that the Indus Valley civilization actually commenced only a few hundred years after the locals in that area began growing crops. As they gradually began to improve their agricultural skills, the people started to lose interest in moving from one place to another, as they had found new means of livelihood other than hunting. The soil being extremely fertile, gave a solid boost and encouraged people to continuously find new ways and means of farming. However, as time went by, the land began to dry out and became less and less capable of producing. But soon the need was felt, and qualified designers and planners began to channelize the supply of water, which enabled them to get rid of water scarcity other than during the monsoon season.

These irrigation channels were generally made of stones, and some of the channels are still in existence even today. Without these water systems, farmers would have had no option, but to migrate in order to maintain their lifestyle and line of activity. This would have triggered the people to move out of the Valley, terminating civilization expeditiously. While agricultural work and farming were the most common, many farmers tended to tame and train animals other than growing plants. Cows and goats were some of the most customary farm animals. While much of the agricultural produce would have been ingested within the Valley, some of it was swapped for other essentials and products of interest with outside nations. It can be conveniently said that farming in the Indus Valley would have continued to exist and flourished without trade, but trade between the Indus Valley and other human settlements would not have been prolonged without an additional quantum of agricultural goods.

The Indus Valley became substantially more densely populated during the mature period than it had been in previous periods. By the mid-2000s BCE, there were over three to four hundred small and large cities and settlements within the Indus Valley. Most of these cities emerged near large rivers and their branches, primarily the Indus. It is important to note that during this period, the major cities of Mohenjo-Daro and Harappa developed rapidly. These cities displayed the superb talent and architectural skills possessed by people.

The occupied land in the Indus Valley was equalized and flattened to facilitate easy transport and building structures. This made construction activity much easier and safer, but the process of flattening wouldn't have been an easy task. Due to this, mounds of rubble and mud cropped up, which gave rise to the disparity. The weaker section of people lived in the lower parts, whereas the richer and mighty occupied higher places.

Houses on the eastern side of the city were comparatively less classy. The western side was mainly occupied by the rich and dignified., which comprised fortified administrative buildings. People in the mature period could be financially and economically distinguished predominantly by the houses occupied by them. Economical and technical advancement was directly related to the different types and architecture of the buildings. As wealth and prosperity grew, the need was felt for building a protective wall around the city, which would not only provide protection and security to its citizens from outside unscrupulous elements, but also from miscreants, and would also protect them from floods during monsoons.

Archaeologists have opined that they couldn't find any significant traces of invasion or use of military force, and they would be right in saying that the walls had served their purpose well. The area occupied by the city and the number of people staying in it was a decisive factor in determining how large the houses would be. Many private houses and buildings were of the same size, with marginally larger homes closer to the higher levels of the cities. This not only shows that the civilization had a comparatively impartial community but also that there was a regulated caliber as to how planners and designers were likely to create new structures. Not very far from houses, cities usually had community halls and markets to fulfill their daily needs. Cities that are nearer or located on the river bank would have seaports. Many of these houses were made out of mud bricks. By this time, set standards were implemented mainly relating to the construction of houses, which helped the identical pattern of buildings. This rewarded the cities for becoming more structured and systematized.

As we see the types of buildings and structures in major cities, we can also get an idea of the quality of life during the integration era. To name a few., public bathhouses were some of the most magnificent structures in any of the cities. Mud and bricks were used to make these quality structures in spite of the fact that their prime purpose was to hold water.

As farming techniques improved, food grain production was abundant. Production was in excess of consumption, hence the need for proper suitable storage facilities was felt. Farmers would keep their grains stored in common places built for the entire local community, known as granaries. Granaries were of prime importance, which is almost comparable to the modern-day farm pit used to store food grains. It ensured that grains were not spoilt, and prevented them from wild animals too. Large cities had larger granaries and excellent storage facilities, wherein the rich had better access and preference. Upon excavation, Archaeologists were able to find disintegrated and crumbled portions of some granaries.

Soon grains were also being used in trade. As a result, large granaries were being built on ports, since the sea was a major mode of transport to different lands. The ports had large and sturdy gates which could be opened and closed conveniently. This prevented the boats from being washed out in storms or floods. Considering the timeline, this was the newest state-of-the-art application of knowledge amongst civilizations globally. Even practices relating to water conservation were excellent, and far ahead of their times. Artificial waterways for inland movement and transport were constructed. Also, storage facilities were built to conserve rainwater. Another accomplishment by the people of the Indus valley was the building of dams. These dams regulated the quantity of water that the area can hold or flow. These, in turn, averted floods, channelized water to different streams, and helped in conserving. Any architectural feat was made with mud and bricks. Any other type of construction material was not used. The Harappans also had conduits, which originated from the high point to the low point finally merging into a large tank or reservoir. Many conduits were channelized into different directions for smooth and effective supplies in cities. With all of these diverse methodologies, it appears that maximum citizens of the valley had direct means to approach water. Later on, as years went by, the supply of water might have decreased due to monsoon shifting to the east. The consequences of this monsoon pattern stemmed the need for relocating from the Indus River Valley and settling in meager and secluded lands.

DEVELOPMENT OF TRADE AND INFRASTRUCTURE

Other than cultivating crops, trading was one of the main lines of activity of people operating in the Indus Valley during the Integration period. Barter exchange was the mechanism used to trade, as there was no concept of currency or any other equivalent medium of exchange.

Trade was conducted both, within a group of people living in the same area, same community, and within people outside the community. This would often involve traveling to distant lands. Initially, trading was conducted mainly in food grains. As farming techniques upscaled and new technologies emerged, production splurged and commodities were produced in excess of consumption. This resulted in finding new avenues for trade and discovering new lands and settlements, which gave rise to efficient means of travel and transport. Most of the travel was thru waterways rather than land, as the former was easy, preferable, and suitable to its geographical location. Due to this, cities began to develop alongside the river. Most of the large towns and cities were consolidated and concentrated along a river, a river's side stream, or a sea. But this also had a negative effect. The location of the Indus valley was such, that it was separated by mountains and valleys from the outer world. As far as land routes were concerned, the citizens of the Indus valley began to detach and were singled out. Excellent water transport methods were developed which facilitated trade. The city of Harappa was a classic example of having high-tech dockyard facilities.

One of the early ages ports in the Indus Valley was at Lothal and rangpur. These docks were built sometime during the 2000s BCE. Most of the other primeval docks found in the Indus Valley are known to have been built many years later. The disintegrated remains of the dockyard at Lothal can still be seen today. Irrespective of their methods and means of transportation, it is quite astonishing to note how they traveled with little equipment and little knowledge of navigation systems. A large chunk of foreign trade happened in Mesopotamia. New trading routes and trade were also developed with the western world., but it wasn't sizable. Artifacts pertaining to the Indus valley period could be found in distant lands, which proves the above. Similarly, artifacts of these faraway places were also found in the Indus valley, establishing the fact that some kind of trade or exchange happened between them. Edible products were some of the most commonly traded items. The Indus valley people not only sold raw goods but also sold processed equipment and stuff made from animals. Clothes, spices, and other products were some of the most regularly traded agricultural products. Articles made of clay or mud such as pots, dishes, and toys were also very popular trading commodities. In later years, as trade began to develop and flourish, Indus valley people created jewelry pieces made of stone and beads. Jewelry was very widely accepted by other nations and soon it became the most highly tradable and popular commodity in international trade. The quality and the value of these products depended on how artistically it was made. Since there was no currency in those times, its cash value in modern times cannot be assessed.

During the mature period, the quality and quantity in craft and jewelry making upscaled and triggered off to extraordinary levels. As new techniques evolved, people began to show great interest in jewelry, which increased demand. The Harappan people developed their metallurgy skills and started using metals, mainly bronze, in articles of day-to-day use. They began using metals for decoration and making toys and sculptures. The use of beads and stones of various colors and shapes in jewelry and decorating articles were already developed to its fullest and were rampant. Glazing and polishing the pieces was done to make things look artistic and increase their value. The use of sea shells in various crafts and decorative showpieces was well known.

Shells were usually not modified but kept in their original shape in order to add to art pieces. But stones, however, were chiseled and altered in various ways to make beautiful sculptures and other fine art pieces. Shells were most likely used in jewelry. Clay and terracotta were widely used to make pottery and other household articles, but their production in bulk and quality improved during the mature period. Designs on pottery used commonly were of animals and people. It was also found that people started using symbols and markings of various shapes and sizes in day-to-day activities in the mature period. However, historians are not able to decode them. Some three to four hundred characters have been found by now. It is presumed that these symbols might represent words or concepts rather than alphabets., and could be some sort of writing language. There is a strong possibility that these symbols or words can give us an idea about the religion being practiced by them. It also shows a connection between the symbols and artwork of those times. Most of the paintings and characters portray animals rather than Gods or goddesses. But there is available information indicating the female Goddess being worshipped, which is similar to the one worshipped in other civilizations of the same period. One of the symbols is very much identical to Lord Pashupati, an incarnation of Lord Shiva. Pashupati is also known as the god of animals, and this seal was found in excavations of Mohenjo Daro in 1929-30 by the Archaeological Survey of India.

LATE HARAPPAN PERIOD
1800 BCE TO 1400 BCE

At the beginning of this phase, the Indus Valley Civilization was at its pinnacle, most powerful, and had covered the maximum area possible. However, from around 1800 BCE, the culture began a slow decline.

The late Indus period saw too much swing, reaching its zenith in trade and commerce and then a decline until its disappearance. The Indus Valley civilization started losing its glory sometime around 1700 BCE and continued until it disappeared around 1300 BCE. Historians have different theories on how and why this happened. One of the reasons we can attribute to the fall is trade. A significant chunk of business was with Mesopotamia. The Indus people were not involved in major wars or battles, so they had good and fruitful relationships with their trading partners. They established excellent and sizable businesses with various groups of people within Mesopotamia.

MESOPOTAMIA—MAJOR TRADE PARTNER

As time went on, the Harappans and Mesopotamians' relationship strengthened. Between 2100 BCE and 1700 BCE, people in business from the Indus Valley built temporary houses and residences in Mesopotamia to store the leftover merchandise that did not sell. This would help them save transportation costs and unnecessary shipping goods to and fro.

Historians found more evidence of Harappan merchants residing temporarily in Mesopotamia than in other areas. Archaeologists have found beads, artifacts, sculptures pottery, in the Harappan style. In Eshnunna, a major city in Mesopotamia, the drainage and sewer system was very much similar to the ones found in Harappa and Mohenjo-Daro. Harappans might have provided them with the necessary technology and know-how. The Harappans and Mesopotamians traded everything from timber to metal and gems to live animals. Out of all of these, raw metal and gemstones were some of the most popular trade items in Mesopotamia. Most of these items were sourced directly from the Indus Valley and then taken to be traded within Mesopotamia.

Let's look at what kind of goods the Indus Valley people traded with the Mesopotamians. Perhaps one of the most commonly traded gemstones was carnelian and lapiz lazuli. Carnelian stones were mined in the Indus Valley. Once exchanged, they were often used to make beads and other artwork and jewelry. Another famous stone was lapis lazuli, a reasonably rare gem. This stone was also primarily used for jewelry and artwork. Copper was also traded often, but it is most likely that the Harappans got their copper by trading with other nations, most likely the people from Magan or civilizations that lived in modern-day India. These goods were traded as raw materials and as finished goods too. Finished goods are those which are ready for sale or exchange. Their valve would have been more than raw goods. Apart from raw materials and handicrafts, trade was abundant in organic materials as agricultural technology flourished in the late Harappan period. Sesame, sesame oil, and wood were traded with Mesopotamians. Timber was a significant product and was in great demand, as it was used to make boats, furniture, and other decorative articles. Woodcraft and other items of daily use were made by the Indus people and traded.

Historians firmly believe the Indian/Harappan trade relationship lasted between 1900 and 1800 BCE. This period was determined by the radiocarbon dating of items found in India and the Indus Valley. These dates line up almost perfectly with the beginning of the Late Harappan period. In spite of the Indus people having excellent and high-volume trade with India, historians need to learn more about it. This is due to a lack of written historical records (that historians can read) and abundant archaeological evidence.

It is also known that the Indus people traded with Mesopotamia, India, and distant places as far as china. Ancient Chinese historians and merchants wrote about conducting trade in the Indus Valley. However, they refer to the area as "Shendu" and "Sindh". With all of this written evidence, historians know more about the Indus Valley trade with China than with India. The Chinese merchants likely did most of the preliminary work regarding traveling. By the late Indus period, the Chinese had already created detailed trade routes across western Asia and parts of the modern-day Middle East. Harappa became a vast and significant trading center for almost all its trading partners, including China. The Chinese merchants undoubtedly had an impact on Harappan society. While historians do not know for sure, it is possible the Chinese influenced the Indus script, as both scripts use characters instead. Historians do not have much information regarding items of trade between China and the Harappans. The Chinese brought jade and cedarwood to exchange in trade with gemstones, beads, wood crafts, and artwork made of native Indus valley materials.

With all of the evidence indicating that the Indus valley was a central trade hub and the fact that merchants could travel to distant places for business, it can be said that the Indus Valley people were a peaceful group who had no "natural" enemies, not because of their geographical status but because of their friendly relationships with nearby nations. They didn't have any class distinction., as there was no difference in the level of treatment among themselves. This can be concluded from the fact that they did not have a centralized administrative body. The buildings were small and large, and none could be identified as a palace or executive office. This was one of the prime factors for peace and harmony prevailing in that period. One of the most significant factors that point to the Indus Valley people being peaceful is their assumed lack of a centralized government. While some homes were more prominent than others in cities, archaeologists have not been able to pinpoint any one building as a temple or palace. A lack of these buildings points to a lack of class disparity, which most would see as a good thing. Not having any solid proof of a centralized government also hints toward the theory that the Indus Valley people might have had city-states. Of course, historians can't be sure of this, as they could not read any Indus valley script that could figure out what their government was like. Many of the smaller cities in the Indus Valley did not have a great defensive wall or other reinforcement built to strengthen the city's boundaries.

Historians and archaeologists failed to find evidence of any defense or military establishment. This shows that the Indus valley people were not afraid of outside forces. There were no weapons that could kill or harm human beings. Whatever type of weapons they had were used only for hunting. There were no security concerns or threats amongst the people., hence they were able to focus more on town planning and sanitation systems. There is no proof that the Indus valley cities might have been attacked, looted, or destroyed at any time. Instead, the Harappans were great at avoiding conflicts, something that is nearly unheard of for any ancient civilization.

Travel and transport within the cities were primitive. Most of it was by surface. They usually walked short distances and used carts for transporting goods, driven by donkeys. Domestic animals were few and ridable. They traveled fearlessly without any concern or threat of being looted or robbed. There were no defined roads, but they were easy to navigate. Long distances and trade with outside civilizations were thru waterways. There is enough evidence that the Harappans had large boats capable of carrying several people and merchandise. As mentioned earlier, the Harappans had excellent trade relations with Mesopotamians and other tribes of India eastwards. As significant cities developed on river banks, large dockyards were built to facilitate trade. Over time, the Harappans had mastered the art of shipbuilding, making it capable of navigating rough waters and traveling great distances.

POLITICAL AND SOCIAL STRUCTURE

Historians cannot identify how exactly the political and administrative structure was in the Indus valley. The script and writings of the Indus people could not be deciphered; as a result, the methodology could not be defined. However, more needs to be found out about the Indus valley administrative machinery. Since historians cannot read the Indus script, there is little proof of how exactly the Indus Valley government was structured. However, certain aspects of Harappan culture and cities hint at the Indus Valley having some government.

Indus Valley Seals

Logically speaking, town planning and development are not possible without having administrative machinery in place. Some type of regulatory body might have been formed to ensure law and order, and efficient administration. Some factor that leads us to determine standardization is the construction pattern devised. Most of the bricks were almost the same size and shape. Even their weights have been consistent.

Large cities in the Indus Valley were more or less organized in the same way as each other. Parts of cities were often leveled and terraced to create man-made changes in elevation. Farmers and other average people likely lived on the lower elevations, while the citadel, other large buildings, and perhaps the richer members of society lived at higher elevations. All of these buildings had to be constructed by someone. And since so many buildings were uniform in shape and size and used the same materials, it is unlikely that no one was regulating the architects, even in the early years of the Indus Valley civilization. Also, let's not forget about the intricate grid patterns that were used throughout most of the larger cities in the Indus Valley. The roads and buildings were placed in such a way that the cities were full of right angles, making traveling and locating buildings easier.

However, this culture started to decline by 1700 BCE. This period was not only a period of de-urbanization; it was also a time when the use of some of the major Indus cities changed. For example, Mohenjo-Daro excavations have shown that the central part of the city, sometimes called the citadel, which appears to have previously been occupied by high-status residences, was turned over to use by artisans, particularly potters. This strongly suggests a significant change in the social order of the city. In his book Indus Civilization (1935), renowned archaeologist Ernest Mackay notes: "This quarter of Mohenjo-Daro, if not the whole of the city, must by this time have declined greatly in social standing and organization, for it is difficult to imagine that the city authorities ... would have allowed potters to practice their craft within the confines of the city."

Many of the new settlements which were established during this tenure were more in the east of the region, namely the Ganga-Yamuna plains. many towns and cities vanished altogether in this period. In the Mature Harappan Phase, there were 175 settlements in the Bahawalpur region, close to the Hakra River. By the middle of the Late Harappan Phase, there were just 50. Other cities were reduced in size.

Lothal

There seems to have been a general shift from large urban centers towards smaller, newer areas of rural communities, which suggests a casual movement of the population. During the mature Harappan phase, even the ceramics, pottery, and handicrafts changed. During this phase, a great deal of pottery and handicrafts were produced, which featured a different style with bold designs on colorful backgrounds.

Products of high value such as sculptures, jewelry, terracotta figures, and detailed ivory-embedded pieces of different expensive materials found at earlier sites are also absent in locations of the late period. Excavations have found that during this period people living in cities began to hide their valuables under the floors of their homes which was never seen before. This resulted in a fragmented social order, fearing robbery and looting, which never happened earlier. In the late period, archaeologists found out that some bodies were left unburied after their death. To summarize, it is clear that some rudimentary changes happened in the Indus Valley, which started somewhere around 1700 BCE. The urbanization and careful planning of towns and cities which had gone before declined and the advanced techniques in construction and architecture seemed to be forgotten. Even sanitation and waste disposal methods, which were an integral part of every previous city were discarded.

SOCIAL STRUCTURE AND HARAPPAN MYTHOLOGY

Historians could not determine if the Indus people had any political or social organization. There were no colonial buildings, community halls, or designated meeting areas where they could form a directorate or regulatory body to govern people. However, the absence of any administrative board or authority is highly unlikely. As the Indus script could not be read and understood, most opinions are based on assumptions and speculations. However, certain aspects, such as the standardization of bricks, their consistent weights, and ratios of Harappan culture and cities, hint at the Indus Valley having some regulatory or administrative body.

It is unknown if the Harappans followed or believed in any religion since historians cannot read the Indus script. Because of this, historians need to use artifacts the Harappans left behind, namely sculptures and other types of artwork. Historians also look at what the people in nearby areas believed in. This is because civilizations with similar cultures may have had equal or shared religions. If the Harappans shared a belief with any other culture, it would most likely have been with the Mesopotamians. Archaeologists have found a sculpture similar to the Mesopotamian mother goddess. If the Harappans worshiped the mother goddess, then it is possible they may have honored some of the other Mesopotamian gods and goddesses, along with following different aspects of their religion. The Mesopotamians had a polytheistic religion, meaning they worshiped more than one god or goddess. The first two gods, Apsu and Tiamat, created the world. Once the world was created, other gods and goddesses came to life. However, these younger gods and goddesses often were in conflict with their elders. Their battles and fallout served to create various features of the earth. These stories worked their way into Mesopotamia's general mythology. As with many other ancient cultures, their mythology shaped the way they saw the world around them and interacted with it. Temples were erected as places to show reverence to the gods and goddesses. If humans worshiped their gods and made sacrifices, the gods would watch over and protect them.

Humans could also pray as a form of worship. However, the Harappans did not build any lavish temples or other buildings that might have been places of worship. This works against the theory that the Harappans and Mesopotamians had the same religion. Then again, they may have worshiped the same gods differently. The Mesopotamians also believed in the power of seeking knowledge of the future or the unknown. The specialists of these skills could interpret messages from the gods by looking at the organs of certain animals, the actions of living animals, and the health of people.

Predicting and reading the future was a specialized skill that not everyone could do. The Harappans may have believed in form of animism. Generally speaking, animism is the belief that all living things have a soul. This worship primarily revolves around animals and plants but can also include rivers and mountains. People chose which plants, animals, departed human spirits, or nonliving objects they wanted to praise. Some archaeologists indicate that the Harappans were animists because they created so many pieces of artwork and seals that display and represent plants and animals. Some of their art pieces showed humans and animals together. Archaeologists also opine that the Harappans believed that stones had spirits in them. It is not known how these animals, plants, and nonliving objects were worshiped. To understand how it might have been done, we need to look at how animism is being followed in other cultures around the globe. The theory that the Harappans were animists holds more weightage than the idea that they worshiped in the exact same way as the Mesopotamians. Religious beliefs don't require any temples or religious leaders. This assumption of the archaeologists suits well with the idea that the Indus Valley didn't have any religious buildings and didn't have any centralized religion. Some animists believed in a supreme god that ruled over all spirits, while other groups did not. In either case, the average animist would have been more concerned with praising and respecting familiar spirits rather than a supreme god. These spirits could affect people on a personal level. If a person disrespected or showed any kind of disbelief in the spirits, they would face bad luck.

Another popular theory is that the Harappans were some of the earliest Hindus or that their religious practices inspired what would eventually become Hinduism. It is tricky to know for sure. Historians estimate that Hinduism as an organized religion started sometime between 2300 BCE and 1500 BCE, most likely in the Indus Valley. While this timeline coincides with the Harappan civilization, it doesn't necessarily mean that everybody in the Harappan culture believed in Hinduism. The Rig Veda, the first of the Hindu holy books, was written sometime around 1400 BCE. There were no traces of any literature in Sanskrit. Hence we can say that the Indus people did not develop Sanskrit as a language. As the Rig Veda is in Sanskrit, we know the Indus Valley people did not write it.

One more important reason to believe the connection of the Harappans to Hinduism is the Pashupati seal. This seal represents a god who was the lord of animals. Historians see this as a proto-Shiva, who is a Hindu god. So, while the Harappans may not have necessarily been Hindu, they may have had a very similar religion to Hinduism. Another reason to substantiate the above is the figures, shapes, and designs representing different concepts or people. Regarding the Indus people, most of their design patterns have been found on seals and pottery. The designs were usually painted on or etched into the work. Various historians and anthropologists have different theories on what these figures could mean. Some of the most common representations in Harappan art were domestic animals. Agriculture was the primary and essential activity of the Indus people; hence domestic animals were an important part of their culture. Animals were a part of their families, and various art forms depicted their importance. Symbols and signs depicting animals were also found on the walls and buildings. This would also help in identifying designated areas for animal trade. Historians have also found that animal sacrifice has been a religious practice in Harappan culture.

Stars were also crucial to the Indus people, as they appeared in their art forms. This indicates that the Harappan appreciated stars mainly for their beauty. However, the importance of stars for astrological reasons could not be ascertained., as very few and highly skilled people had knowledge about astronomy., and astronomy and predicting the future was at an elementary stage. Various shapes and symbols were also used to represent ideas and concepts. This was the basis of forming some script that could be read and understood by all. Vedic astrology has its roots in the Indus Valley and began about 300 BCE. While this was a considerable amount of time after the Indus Valley civilization had ended, it is possible that the Vedics held some of the same astrological views as the Harappans. If the Harappans believed in some early form of astrology, it likely would not have been as complex as the later Vedic astrology.

Fish were another common symbol used by them. Unlike domesticated farm animals, fish were more likely to represent gods, religion, or the stars. Other line markings or shapes near the fish might have meant a specific star, a number of stars, or planets. These same symbols would later be adopted by the Vedics. This suggests that the Harappans had an interest in astrology and that they could have influenced some aspects of Vedic astrology.

DECLINE AND COLLAPSE OF THE CIVILIZATION

In the earlier chapters, we learned that the Indus Valley people stayed away from war, invasion, and other threats from other nations. This could have mainly been due to their healthy trade relationships with nearby nations or because of the mountain ranges surrounding the Indus Valley, which would have made it difficult to invade. Unlike many other civilizations, which came to an end because of war or invasion, its culture faded and declined slowly. It is challenging to assess the exact cause of the decline. Still, a shift in agricultural patterns could have been a significant factor for the inhabitants to move out and look for greener pastures elsewhere.

Many historians have different opinions as to what led to the collapse of the Indus Valley Civilization. There are four main theories as to what may have happened: climate change, a sudden termination of outside trade links, a change in the course of the Indus River, or an invasion. Let's look at these in turn.

CHANGE IN WEATHER CONDITIONS

During the Indus Valley Civilization, there is some evidence that the region close to the Indus River became increasingly dry or barren to support vegetation. The main reason is a shift in the area where the monsoon rains occurred. As this culture grew and expanded, there is evidence that the monsoon gradually increased and moved to the east. The regular overwhelming of people caused by the monsoon kept the land close to the major cities fertile, without the need to build complex irrigation systems. However, if the monsoon continued to move to the east, the land close to the Indus River would have become less productive. It would have been unable to produce the food surpluses needed to support the populations of large urban centers. This would also impact trade since the surplus agricultural produce was a major trade commodity between Harappans and other nations. Historians who accept this cause for the decline of the Indus Valley Civilization suggest that this explains why large segments of the population seemed to migrate towards the east and the Ganges Basin. However, the new farming land was less fertile than the land close to the Indus River had been and did not produce the food surpluses needed to support the workforce required to build new cities or continue trade with other cultures. In that sense, climate change in the form of gradual aridification accounts for the gradual decline of the Indus Valley Civilization and explains why the population has migrated to the east. Evidence of large-scale flooding has been found at Mohenjo-Daro,

Kalibangan, and Dholavira. In each case, archaeologists have found collapsed buildings and streets covered in silt clay which have subsequently been built on.

In Mohenjo-Daro, serious flooding might have happened at least three to four times. Even the city of Chanhudaro appears to have been completely destroyed by an extensive overabundance of flooding on at least two to three occasions. Recently even in 2010, flooding continued to be a serious problem in this area. In that year, the Harappan archaeological site at Jognakhera was immersed under more than ten feet of water, while the Sutlej Yamuna link canal overflowed. Flooding on this scale would also have had a significant effect on agriculture, perhaps causing food shortages and forcing people to move away from these areas. There is no one common opinion amongst historians on what could have caused this periodic and massive flooding, though some have suggested tectonic events may have created a temporary natural dam to stop the flow of the Indus River before this was somehow released to cause flooding downstream.

The Indus Valley civilization depended mainly on the monsoon seasons to know when to plant and harvest their crops. Without being able to rely on this seasonal schedule, Harappan farmers would have struggled to grow enough food. Drought was one of the major problems that could have happened. A recent 2018 archaeological study suggests the Indus Valley went through a major drought season that lasted almost nine hundred years. This would have started sometime around 2300 BCE and lasted until about 1400 BCE. This timeline matches well with the period of decline and the end of the Indus Valley civilization. Just because the drought season lasted about nine hundred years, it doesn't mean there were no monsoons or rain for that entire time. Instead, the monsoon rains were not as expected and were highly unpredictable. As a result, civilization weakened over the centuries. The researchers who discovered this drought period suggested that the Harappans would have moved out of the Indus Valley to look for more fertile land. It is possible that the Harappans moved eastwards, to the Ganga-Yamuna Valley, Bengal, and Vindhyachal. Of course, it is likely that many Harappans would have starved to death before the civilization as a whole broke apart and moved to other areas, mostly to modern-day India.

Although the monsoons may have been weaker in the last millennium, the Indus Valley was still prone to flooding. An archaeological expedition in the mid-1960s showed that some Harappan buildings were artificially raised over many years, most likely to increase the buildings above rising water levels. Floodwaters that were high enough to be a threat to buildings would also have likely damaged farms and destroyed crops. The same expedition opined that some floodwater deposits were raised about almost twenty-five feet above where the water levels usually were.

Scientists will likely study the building styles in the future to give us a better guess at when the buildings were raised, which would also give us a good estimate of when the floods happened. Flooding occurred many times., and was a significant cause of concern to the Harappans. Just as the monsoon season went in unperiodic and haphazard cycles, so did the floods. Historians suggest there could have been up to six major floods in the Indus Valley before the civilization's end. Similar to the drought situation, the Harappans would have likely moved out of the Indus Valley to avoid the effects of these floods.

CESSATION OF TRADE

Around 2200 BCE, climatic change had a highly destructive and damaging effect on the Akkadian Empire in Mesopotamia. Excavations at the Akkadian city of Shekhna showed not only that the city was abandoned around this time but that all signs of life in the earth itself, including earthworms, vanished for almost 300 years. Research suggests that this was caused by a drop in the surface temperature of the North Atlantic and which led to disruption in the flow and regular flooding of the Tigris and Euphrates Rivers. However, the effects of this event were felt well beyond Mesopotamia. The River Nile was also affected, and the Old Kingdom of Egypt, which had lasted for more than 500 years, was suddenly destroyed by a wave of famines and subsequent social breakdown. Even on the Arabian Peninsula, the Umm al-Nar Culture, which had been in existence for hundreds of years, suddenly vanished. Mesopotamia, Pharaonic Egypt and the Arabian Peninsula had all been major trading partners for the Indus Valley Civilization, and suddenly all three were no longer viable destinations for exports or a source of imports. There has been speculation that this culture had become dependent on imports and exports to such an extent that the sudden removal of most trading partners led to the collapse and eventual abandonment of major cities.

CHANGE IN THE COURSE OF THE INDUS RIVER

Geological surveys have shown that the Indus River has changed its course several times. This may have been due to silt build-up, causing the creation of natural dams and diverting the river flow. Tectonic events could have also caused it, as the Indus River Valley is seismically highly active. During the period from 8000 to 4000 BCE, the Indus River had two separate courses, with the Jacobabad course on the western edge of the valley and the Nara River running parallel on the eastern edge of the plains. During the period from 4000 to 2000 BCE, the two rivers gradually shifted more towards the east. Mohenjo-Daro was initially located between the two rivers, and as they changed course, they might have ceased to support or might have completely given up. Smaller rivers, such as the Ravi and the Beas, also changed course several times. Archaeological evidence shows that Indus settlements were first occupied and then abandoned as the rivers moved. It certainly seems possible that changes in the course of rivers on which the agriculture of the Indus Valley Civilization was so dependent may have had an alarming effect on individual settlements and even cities.

FOREIGN INVASION

As the awareness about the civilization grew in the 1920s, there was a widespread assumption that an invasion from outside the region caused the destruction of this culture. One of the first academic books about this civilization, The Indus Civilization, was written in 1953 by British historian and archaeologist Sir Mortimer

Wheeler. The book suggested and assumed that the existence of the culture was destroyed following an invasion by Aryan migrants from central Asia who arrived with well-organized armies and advanced weapons and conquered the peaceful Harappans. Wheeler could say this because he discovered many unburied dead bodies in some cities. Wheeler combined this with a reading of the Rigveda, an ancient Indian Vedic Sanskrit text that forms one of the four Vedas of Hinduism. These texts mention a war between incoming Aryans and the local inhabitants of the Indus Valley.

It has also been noted that the Harappan culture had disappeared entirely by 1400 BCE, whereas the Rigveda was not written until 300 years later, around 1100 BCE. So, the Rigveda cannot be taken as a contemporary account. It is instead a historical account managed and directed by myth. Finally, many anthropologists have noted that if another culture had conquered the Indus Valley Civilization from the outside, there would have been an unavoidable integration of crafts and social structure, which should be immediately visible and have been understood in recovered artifacts. However, nothing of this sort has been discovered. For these reasons, the theory that an invasion destroyed the Indus Valley Civilization is primarily disregarded. Finally, it can be concluded that there was no single cause for the decline of the Indus Valley Civilization. There could have been a combination of factors, which include environmental changes combined with declining trade, which led to a process of de-urbanization. As the Vedic culture began to emerge in Punjab around 1200 BCE with its own distinctive language, ideology, and social order, it supported and absorbed the fragmented remains of the Indus Valley Civilization.

INTEGRATION INTO THE ARYAN CULTURE

As the Indus Valley civilization ended gradually, it resulted in the Harappans leaving the area and moved in search of better pastures. As mentioned, most Harappans likely moved into modern-day India and the surrounding areas. When the Harappans moved, they probably intermarried and had children with the native people from these areas. There are a few different theories about which cultures the Harappans might have assimilated with. While the Aryan invasion theory has been more or less discredited, it is possible that the Harappans mixed into the Aryan culture. The Aryans migrated to modern-day India and Pakistan around 1600 BCE to 1500 BCE. This also lines up with the decline and fall of the Indus Valley civilization's timeline. There is no evidence of any war or battle with the Aryans in the Indus Valley. Genetic evidence proves that the Aryans were present in India. Research shows Aryan ancestry in genetic data all around India. This indicates that the Aryans did go into India, where they likely would have come into contact with the Harappans. The presence of Harrapans is debatable, whether they migrated from modern-day Pakistan into modern-day India. This is primarily due to a lack of written evidence. One historian, Richard Meadow, argues that no documentation from any group shows the Harappans moved into southern India. Apparently, old Tamil poems talk about migration from the northwest of India to the east of India. He also suggests that if a large-scale migration happened, it likely would have been overland instead of any other means of transport. Any wooden boats or organic material they used on their journey would have been long biodegraded. There is also debate on whether or not the Harappans and Vedics had anything to do with each other. The movement of people described in the Rig Veda does not align with the sedentary and inactive lifestyle of the Harappan people. On top of this, religion was critical to the Vedics, and historians still do not know which religion the Harappans followed or if they even followed any. On the other hand, archaeologists have found Harappan seals depicting Pashupati, a proto-Hindu version of Shiva. It could also indicate that the Vedics adopted some Harappan religious values. The most likely way this would have happened is if the Harappans assimilated with the Aryans at some point. The seals are not the only signs that the Indus Valley civilization had some impact on the Vedics. Some other Harappan ideas and practices were adopted by the Aryans, such as using fire altars, taking ritual baths, and admiration and fondness for the stars. Most likely, the Harappans (or ancestors of the Harappans) and the Aryans came into contact with each other at some point. Their cultures and lifestyles mixed up with each other. Eventually, the Harappan civilization slowly began to dismantle and merge into the Aryan culture.

CHAPTER 2
THE VEDIC PERIOD

INTRODUCTION

The Vedic Period, also known as the Aryan period, existed in the later phase of the Indus Valley Civilization. The word "Arya" means noble in Sanskrit. The Aryans were a group of people who shared common attitudes, interests, and goals and believed in sacrifices and activities prescribed by traditions. The term Aryan is found in the Avesta, the religious text of Zorastrians, which has the same meaning. The term Arya or Aryans is found in the literary works of Megasthenes., the Greek writer and historian, who was also an ambassador of Selucas Nikator 1 in the court of Chandragupta Maurya. He visited India in the 3rd century BCE., and is well known for his book "Indica." To enable a detailed study of the Vedic period and culture., it is essential to study the four Vedas and other Vedic pieces of literature, which I will cover later in this section.

As discussed in the earlier chapters, the Harappan culture and the mighty Sarasvati River began declining after 1000-900 BCE. Indeed, this was not a mere concurrence of events. The crucial factors responsible for the decline are vital in the disappearance of people who built Harappa and Mohenjo-Daro, which include earthquakes, floods, and the lack of warfare technology. Likely for all these reasons, the people who fabricated their societies around the Sarasvati and Indus Rivers dumped their cities and dwindled into the background of aesthetic appeal they had once dominated. As the culture died, a new one moved in with a group of northwestern and central Asians: the Aryans. The Aryans, a group of wandering people, did not overtake the cities, but they probably settled peacefully over their land with their cattle, looking for where their animals could be fed. There are no written records of what occurred during this phase of India's history. Also, there is no physical evidence of any sort of combative and warlike takeover. The fusion of Aryans with the locals gave rise to cooperation and respect. Many researchers believe that it was the Aryan people, and not the original inhabitants of Harappan culture, who wrote the Vedic texts that would continue to become Hinduism's most important literature. This calculation and opinion was based on archaeological and cultural evidence from the Harappan sites. So, logically speaking, it was the Aryans who wrote the first Vedic scriptures and not the Indigenous Indians who developed this important belief system. Practically and feasabily, it may be opined that there was a mixed influence of the Harrapans and Aryans, who came together to create the Vedas just as peacefully as they came together to share the land.

The Aryans, or Indo Aryans as we may call them, belonged to the Indo-European tribe that crossed the Hindu Kush mountain range during the 5th century BC and gradually settled in and alongside the Saptha Sindhu region. In the present day, this region mainly lies in northern Afghanistan and Pakistan. The Aryans were initially wanderers and nomadic people living in the plains, primarily from central Asia. However, different historians have different views about the origin of Aryans.

One of the brazen misconceptions that have been forced upon the hegemonized Indian frame of mind, mainly by the European community, is the European and Christian missionaries' version of the Aryan Invasion Theory (AIT). The missionaries and foreigners say that the Aryans came from foreign lands, snatched the lands of the locals., and annihilated them. They had unscrupulous and mean intentions behind framing this theory. It is bizarre to note that some categories of our Indian scholars support this claim, and this rubbish is taught officially in the prescribed history textbooks in our schools and colleges to young students.

Various historians have discussed the theory of Aryan origin in depth from time to time. However, the majority of scholars believe that Aryans lived in West Asia and Central Asia. European scholars trace Aryan origin to Europe, whereas Indian scholars claim that Aryans have been Indians since time immemorial. Linguistic similarity is also a significant factor in determining the origin of Aryans.

Prof. Maxmuller, a German linguist, used the linguistic similarity of Indo-European languages to conclude Aryan origin in Central Asia. According to him, Sanskrit, Latin, Greek, Persian, and English are similar and have a common origin. To quote some examples:- The Sanskrit word "Pitru" is identical to the Greek word "Pitar". The Sanskrit word "Matru" resembles the Greek "Metar". He believed the people who spoke these languages lived in areas ranging from Central Asia to Eastern Europe. With the passage of time, they relocated and moved from one place to another to different places in the world, and one such group settled in the Saptha Sindhu region.

Indian scholars and writers like R.D. Pandey and D.S. Divedi argued that Aryans were not migrants from a foreign land but were Indians. Ganganath Jha claimed that the Aryans were originally from Brahamarshi land and Multan in Punjab.

Even Rigveda, the oldest and most crucial text among the four Vedas, highlights the religious and social life of Aryans, but it does not mention or support the theory of Aryan migration from foreign lands. Prof. D.N. Jha and Rajaram believe Punjab is the origin of Aryans and not the Middle East. According to L.D. Kalla, Kashmir, and the Himalayan region were the origin of Aryans. There are divergent views on the origin of Aryans, but many scholars upheld the theory of migration from Central Asia.

The earliest Aryans lived in eastern Afghanistan's territory, the North-West Frontier Province, Punjab, and western Uttar Pradesh's outer edges. Some rivers in Afghanistan, such as the Kubha and Indus rivers and their five branches, are mentioned in the Rig Veda. The Sindhu, which has similar boundaries to the Indus, is the main river of the Aryans, and it is mentioned in the Rig Veda. Another river, the Sarasvati, is one of the most important rivers in the Rig Veda.

The entire region where the Aryans first settled in the Indian subcontinent is called the Land of the Seven Rivers. THE 'LAND OF SEVEN RIVERS' or 'SAPTA SINDHU, 'as we may call it, was the new home to the

Aryans. Saptha Sindhu is a land of seven rivers, namely Indus, Saraswati, Vipasa (Bias), Sutudri (Sutlej), Parushni (Ravi), Asikni (Chenab), and Vithasa (Jhelum).

SEVEN RIVERS (SAPTA SINDHU)

Let us discuss the seven rivers (SAPTA SINDHU) in detail:

SINDHU:

The Sindhu River, also known as the Indus River, is one of the largest river basins in the world. It is an essential mode of water transport in South Asia and is also one of the longest rivers in the world, with a total length of over 2,000 miles. It runs from the northeast Kailash Mountain in Tibet, flows through Kashmir, enters Pakistan, and flows south before emptying into the Arabian Sea near Karachi in Pakistan.

The Indus receives its most remarkable tributaries from the eastern Punjab Plain. These five rivers—the Jhelum, Chenab, Ravi, Beas, and Sutlej—give the name Punjab ("Five Rivers") to the region divided between Pakistan and India. This region was home to the ancient Indus Valley Civilization, one of the oldest known civilizations. The Indus Valley Civilization boasted houses with wells and bathrooms, underground drainage systems, a fully developed writing system, impressive architecture, and a well-planned urban center.

SARASWATI:

Rigvedic and later Vedic texts have been used to propose identification with present-day rivers or ancient riverbeds. The Nadistuti hymn in the Rigveda mentions the Sarasvati between the Yamuna in the east and the Sutlej in the west. At the same time, some scholars describe the Sarasvati River as flowing into the Samudra, a word now usually translated as 'ocean.' Later Vedic texts such as the Jayamina Bramhna and the Mahabharata mention that the Sarasvati dried up in a desert.

Since the late 19th century, numerous scholars have proposed identifying the Sarasvati with the Ghagra-Hakka system, which flows through modern-day northwestern India and eastern Pakistan between the Yamuna and the Sutlej and ends in the Thar desert. Recent geophysical research shows that the supposed downstream Ghaggar-Hakra paleochannel is a paleochannel of the Sutlej, which flowed into the River, a delta channel of the Indus River. Around 10,000-8,000 years ago, this channel was abandoned when the Sutlej diverted its course, leaving the Ghaggar-Hakra as a system of monsoon-fed rivers that did not reach the sea.

VIPASA (BEAS):

The Beas River, a tributary of the Indus River, rises in Rohtang Pass in the northwest Himalayas in present-day Himachal Pradesh. It flows south to the Kullu Valley and then west to the Kangra Valley. After crossing the Kangra Valley, it flows into Punjab and merges with

Sutluj. The Beas River was the easternmost border of Alexander's conquest in 326 BC.

SUTUDRI (SUTLUJ):

Satluj is an ancient river, and is one of the tributaries of the Indus River. It is one of the five rivers that give the state of Punjab its name. Satluj enters India near Shipki La Pass, from where it travels across the many Himalayan valleys before integrating with the Beas River in Punjab. After merging with the Beas River, it again merges with Chenab in Pakistan before emptying into the Indus. Many big and small streams amalgamate into Satluj at every step. Traveling along the valleys of Kinnaur district in Himachal Pradesh, along the Satluj River, you will observe several small streams carrying the waters from the freshly melted glaciers to Satluj. The ancient name of the river Sutudri comes from the millions of streams that make the Satluj. The Satluj is quite clamorous and ruthless in monsoon months. It is in rage and looks scary. Many medium and large rocks and stones flow like a small ball in Satluj. The roar of the water as it runs at the base of mighty mountains is all you hear within some distance of the river. This tremendous speed and force of the Satluj makes it perfect for hydropower projects. India's oldest power plant was built on Satluj at Bhakra Nangal. Karcham Wangtoo Hydroelectric Project near the villages of Karcham and Wangtoo stands out in the valley as the only prominent man-made unit surrounded by nature.

In the Chaitra-Ratha Parva of Adi Parva, in Mahabharata, when sage Vasisht wanted to commit suicide, he saw the river named Haimāvata (whose source is Himavat), flooded and full of crocodiles and other aquatic creatures of extraordinary size. So he jumped into the river. Thinking that Vasishtha was a mass of uncontrolled fire, the river widened itself and flew in several directions. Henceforth, the river was named śatadra (or śutudri), a river of hundreds of courses. So, Vasishtha landed on dry land and was unharmed.

PARUSHNI (RAVI)

The Ravi River is a transboundary River of India and Pakistan and an integral part of the Indus River basin. According to the Vedas, the Ravi River was known as Iravati or Parushini. According to the 7th mandala of the Rigveda, the battle of King Sudas and the tribes was fought on the banks of the River Ravi. It rises in Himachal Pradesh, flows northwest past Chamba, and enters Pakistan through Jammu and Kashmir.

ASIKNI (CHENAB):

The confluence of Chandra and Bhaga streams forms the Chenab River. It rises in the Indian state of Himachal Pradesh and flows through Jammu and Kashmir between the steep cliffs of the Sivalik Range and the lesser Himalayas. Turning southwest, it enters Pakistan and empties itself into the Sutluj, a tributary of the Indus.

VITASA (JHELUM):

The Jhelum River flows from the Indian Union territory of Jammu and Kashmir into Pakistani Punjab, passing through the Pakistani-administered territory of Azad Kashmir. It is the westernmost of the Punjab region's five rivers and flows through the Kashmir Valley. It is a

Chenab River tributary with a total length of about 725 kilometers. The Jhelum originates at Vernag, in western Jammu and Kashmir union territory, in the Indian-administered portion of the Kashmir region, from a deep spring. The river flows northwestward from the Pir Panjal Range's northern slope through the Valey of Kashmir to Srinagar's Wular Lake, which regulates its flow. The Jhelum emerges from the lake and flows westward, cutting through the Pir Panjal in a gorge 7,000 feet (2,100 meters) deep gorge with almost perpendicular sides.

The availability of abundant water resources and rich grassland made Aryans settle in the Saptha Sindhu region. The Aryans found this land fertile and capable of producing abundant vegetation. They blended and fused themselves with the locals. This was a time when India gained importance and cultural identity. Aryans bonded with this region to such an extent that the two customs, art, and other manifestations of human intellectual achievement became one, with beliefs and traditions amalgamated and combined to form a single entity. By the 5th century BCE, the Vedic religion began to develop into a structure that more closely resembled Hinduism, though the Vedas remain the central focus of Hinduism today. The people who first read and spoke of them do not bear much resemblance to those who chant the Vedas now; however, the former was largely pastoral people whose livelihoods depended on raising animals for meat and milk.

Agriculture was done using these seven rivers as the primary source of water. Agricultural equipment was made of copper and bronze. But none of these tools were excavated in this region. Archaeological sources in this region link the Rigveda period to the prior period. Many sites were discovered in Punjab, Afghanistan, and belonged to the Rig Vedic Period, but the people followed Harappan culture. They used Harappa pots and OchreColoured Pottery (OCP) found in Mitalal, Bara, and Rupar. OCP symbolizes the mature Chalcolithic age belonging to Harappan culture. Three sites discovered in Bhagavanpur (Haryana) and Punjab belonged to the Rig Vedic Period. Thirteen-room mud houses of a joint family or a tribal leader were found in Bhagavanpur. Here, skeletons of animals were discovered, but there were no traces of Iron. The period was estimated to be between 1400 and 900 BC, which is undoubtedly the Rig Vedic Period.

VEDIC LITERATURE

RIGVEDA MS2097

The word 'Veda' comes from the root 'Vid' (literally, 'to know'), which means knowledge. There are four Vedas- Rigveda, Samaveda, Yajurveda, and Atharvaveda. The Rigveda contains the world's oldest surviving poetry, some of it of extraordinary beauty, devoted to studying fundamental expertise in depth. Each Vedas has four parts: The Samhita, Brahmana, Aranyaka, and Upanishad. The Rigveda Samhita is a collection of 1,028 hymns arranged in 10 books (Mandalas). The Samaveda consists of 1,810 verses, mostly borrowed from the Rigveda, arranged according to the elements and series of written symbols used to represent music. The Yajurveda deals with the details of the rituals and performance. The Atharvaveda is the latest Veda and contains hymns, spells, and charms that reflect features of well-accepted beliefs and practices. The Brahmanas (this term should not be confused with the Brahmana Varna or Caste) are prose explanations of the Vedas that give full particulars and descriptions of sacrificial rituals and the end result. The Aranyakas interpret sacrifices and rituals symbolically and philosophically. There are a hundred Upanishads, among which thirteen are the most important. They contain many philosophical ideas about surrendering possessions or wealth, such as animals, as an offering to God. The body and the universe are most closely associated with the concepts of Atman and Brahman. The Vedic texts comprise devout literature with few references to possible historical events. To cite an example, chapter 7 of the Rigveda Samhita refers to a battle of ten kings in which Sudas defeated several adversaries who had confederated against him. Historians have tried to reconstruct various aspects of the culture represented in the Vedas, but it is not an easy task to interpret this vast and complete literature. Vedic literature forms an essential part of the Brahmanical tradition, preserved and transmitted by a section of Brahmans. It represents their religious beliefs, practices, and points of view. As a source of History, these texts are used for information about life in parts of northwestern and northern India during the 2nd and 1st millennia BCE. A significant hindrance to using the Vedas as a source of history is dating the Rigveda. The dates suggested for the composition by this text range from Circa 6000 BCE to 1000 BCE.

The Rig Veda, one of the oldest revered texts in the Indo-European tradition, offers the capacity to gain an accurate and deep understanding of the early Aryan civilization in India. The term "Arya" appears thirty-four times within its verses, suggesting a well-defined cultural community describing the distinctive nature or features using the Indo-Aryan language. This frequent mention underscores not only their linguistic identity but also indicates the social and cultural values they hold. The Vedas provide a glimpse into the lives, beliefs, and practices of the Aryans, which sheds light on their societal structures, rituals, and interactions with the environment around them, thereby enhancing the quality and value of our understanding of their historical significance in the subcontinent. The Rig Veda is the earliest text of the Indo-European languages. It is a collection of prayers offered to Agni, Indra, Mitra, Varuna, and other gods by various families of poets or sages. It consists of ten mandalas or books, of which books II to VII form the earliest parts. Books I and X seem to have been the latest additions. The Rig Veda has many things in common with the Avesta, which is the oldest text in the Iranian language. The two texts use the same terms for several gods and even for social classes. However, the earliest example of the Indo-European language is found in an inscription from Iraq, written about 2300 BC. Later, such specimens occur in Hittite inscriptions in Anatolia (Turkey) from the nineteenth to the seventeenth centuries BC. They also figure in the Mycenaean inscriptions of Greece around 1500 BC. Aryan names appear in Kassite inscriptions from about 1600 BC in Iraq and Mitanni inscriptions from the fourteenth century BC in Syria. However, so far, no such inscriptions have been found in India. The Aryans migrated to India in several waves. The Rig Vedic people represent the earliest wave, who came to the subcontinent in about 1600-1500 BC.

Hindu tradition believes that the Vedas are "APAURUSEYA," meaning that they are not of human origin but have been made known by the divine for the benefit of all human beings. This belief emphasizes the state of being holy and being the highest authority in Hindu religious and philosophical thought. Thus, the Vedas are considered timeless disclosures to humans that abbreviate spiritual truths, hymns, rituals, and philosophical insights that continue to influence Hindu thoughts and practices.

Veda originated from the word "Vid," meaning to know. So, Veda means knowledge. A book that contains Vedic thoughts is also a Veda. The Vedas constitute the primary scriptures of the Hindus. They constitute the very foundation of Hinduism. Without Vedas, there is no Hinduism. The Vedas are also the fundamental source of other scriptures. The Vedas are the manifestation of Indian wisdom.

The Vedas are regarded as a system of higher understanding that can explain how best to utilize one's present situation. To quote an example., when you buy an appliance or a car, you also get an owner's manual to help explain how to use and take care of it. In the same way, the Vedas were given to people so they may know who they are, how they got here, how this world works, and how to utilize this life to their best advantage and avoid unseen dangers. This is confirmed in the Yajur Veda, which states that God created the Vedas and revealed all things through them. Ultimately, the primary purpose of the Vedic literature is to establish knowledge of spiritual realization and provide a way to attain freedom from suffering. This means getting discharged from materialistic embroilment by using this human form of life to reach (or return to) the spiritual platform of existence. But no matter what level of desires you may have, you have an answer to any questions that may arise in continuing your upliftment and progress. The Vedas teach how to modulate ordinary work and channel that activity into actions that reward the performer with future benefits. As a person's life becomes regulated accordingly, he naturally grows toward a superior stage of philosophical understanding. As one gains more profound enlightenment by practical experience, one also perceives the real purpose of life through the Vedas.

This is explained in the Srimad-Bhagavatam: "Your word in the form of the Veda is the one excellent eye possessed by the ancestors, gods, and human beings, enabling them to obtain insight into the unseen purpose of life, such as final liberation, heavenly bliss, as well as the goal to be attained in this very life and the means of attaining it, O Lord." (Bhag.11.20.4)

The Bhagavad-gita, the most revered text of the Hindus, states: "This knowledge is the king of education, the most secret of all secrets. It is the purest knowledge, and because it gives a direct perception of the self by realization, it is the perfection of religion. It is everlasting and is joyfully performed." (Bg.9.2)

A person who has been covered over by ignorance since time immemorial cannot affect his self-realization; hence, there must be some other personality who has factual knowledge of the Absolute Truth and can impart this knowledge to them." (Bhag.11.22.10) Therefore, we must be watchful and vigilant about whom we approach to understand the Vedic teachings. This means that not only should the teacher be discreetly selected, but you should also choose which interpretation of the Vedas you read. Some scholars, for example, have complained that the Vedas are too vague and unclear. As a result, due to their lack of understanding, they dismiss the Vedic teachings as unimportant. There is a reason for this. It has been said that knowledge in the hands of a covetous person can be perilous. Thus, the Vedas may deal in esoteric terms so that the people tending to obstruct or harm will not understand. As Lord Krishna, the Supreme Being, says in Srimad-Bhagavatam: "The Vedas, divided into three divisions, ultimately reveal the living entity as pure spirit soul. However, the Vedic seers and mantras deal in esoteric terms, and I am also pleased by such confidential descriptions. The transcendental sound of the Vedas is challenging to comprehend and manifests on different levels within the prana (life energy), senses, and mind. This Vedic sound is unlimited, intense, and unfathomable, just like an ocean." (Bhag.11.21.35-36) To explain further, one must practice or participate in the highest levels of Vedic philosophy thoroughly. One can study it to attain a much higher understanding of one's real identity. Still, this type of well-informed learning is limited in its perspective and is typical of the Western approach to researching philosophy. A complete view of Vedic philosophy will increase as one studies and practices the teachings in the Vedic writings. These practices help one develop inner comprehension for a more complete understanding and direct perception of the spiritual information within the Vedas. This is the point and the difference it makes.

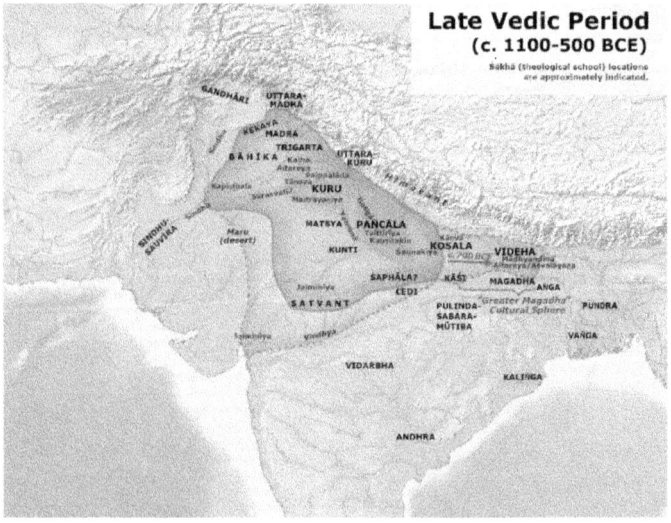

Late Vedic Period (1100-500 BCE)

The Vedas give a clear idea about how this universe was created and how to follow the laws of nature so that we humans can think beyond just eating, sleeping, etc. Other living beings do not understand and study how the world was created and how to be grateful for food, water, and shelter. Human beings are blessed with a higher level of intelligence. Vedas imparts tremendous knowledge in physics, chemistry, math, medical science, art, etc. Vedic scientists started the education system in the world and were called 'RISHIMUNIS".

Not only do the Vedas contain a high level of philosophical and spiritual knowledge, but they also hold information on material science. The Vedic literature includes works such as Ayurveda, the original science of holistic medicine as taught by Lord Dhanvantari; Dhanur-Veda, the military science as taught by Bhrigu; Gandharva-Veda, which is on the arts of music, dance, drama, etc., by Bharata Muni; Artha-sastra, the science of government; Sthapatyaveda, the science of architecture; and the Manu-Samhita, the first lawbook. There is also the Shulba Sutras, which contains the Vedic system of mathematics. These sutras supplement the Kalpasutras, which show the earliest forms of algebra. The Vedic form of mathematics is much more advanced than in early Greek, Babylonian, Egyptian, or Chinese civilizations. The geometrical formula known as the Pythagorean theorem can be traced to the Baudhayana, the earliest form of the Shulba Sutras before the 8th century BCE. It was this Indian system that originated the decimal system of tens, hundreds, etc., and the procedure of carrying the remainder of one column over to the next. It also provided a means of dividing fractions and using equations and letters to signify unknown factors. These Indian numbers were used in Arabia after 700 CE and then spread to Europe, where they were called Arabic numerals. It is only because Europe changed from Roman numerals to Arabic numerals that originated in India that many scientific and math developments took place in Europe. The Puranas contain various information on the creation of the universe, its maintenance, and destruction. Other subjects include astrology, geography, use of military weapons, organization of society, duties of different classes of men, characteristics, and behavior of social leaders, predictions of the future, analysis of the material elements, symptoms of consciousness, how the illusory energy works, the practice of yoga, meditation, spiritual experiences, realizations of the Absolute, and much more. The Vedas, written hundreds of years ago, also completely disproves modern scholars' theory that all ancient civilizations thought the earth was the center of the universe and the stars and sun revolved around it. The Vedic description of the cosmological arrangement explains that all planets, as well as the sun, have their particular orbits of travel through the universe.

According to Hindu tradition, the Vedas were not composed by any author or group of authors but were revealed to ancient sages (rishis) through divine inspiration or revelation. This process is known as "Shruti," which means "that which is heard" in Sanskrit. The belief is that these sages, during deep meditation or spiritual experiences, received the hymns and verses directly from the cosmic consciousness or the divine realm. Here's a general understanding of how the Vedas were transmitted according to Hindu tradition:

RISHIS AND THEIR DISCLOSURES:

Ancient sages, known as rishis, were seers deeply receptive to spiritual knowledge and meditation. Through tapa (austerity) and spiritual practices, they attained states of consciousness and received profound insights and wisdom.

ORAL TRANSMISSION:

Initially, the Vedas were transmitted orally from the teacher (guru) to the disciple (shishya). This oral tradition ensured that the texts were preserved accurately over generations.

PRESERVATION AND COMPILATION:

Certain rishis and scholars compiled these hymns and verses into collections over time. This process is believed to have occurred over centuries, with the Rigveda being the oldest and the other Vedas following subsequently.

As mentioned earlier, the Vedas are ancient texts that form the core of Hinduism. It is challenging to determine the exact dates of the compilation of the Vedas. They are composed in Vedic Sanskrit and are classified into four main collections:

THE RIGVEDA: The Rigveda is the oldest sacred text of ancient Indian civilization and is considered one of the oldest religious texts in the world. It is a collection of hymns and spiritual texts in Vedic Sanskrit, dating back to around 1500–1200 BCE, though some parts may be older. The Rigveda is a foundational Hindu text and one of the four Vedas, the primary scriptures of Hindu philosophy and ritual. The Rigveda consists of 1,028 hymns (suktas) divided into ten books called Mandalas. These hymns are dedicated to various deities such as Agni (the god of fire), Indra (the king of gods and god of thunder and rain), Varuna (the god of sky and water), and many others. The hymns praise the gods, explore the relationship between humanity and the divine, and discuss rituals and philosophical ideas. In addition to its religious significance, the Rigveda provides valuable insights into ancient India's culture, society, and language. It has been preserved through an oral tradition for centuries before being written down in Sanskrit. The Rigveda continues to be studied and revered in Hinduism, and its hymns are still recited in religious ceremonies and rituals today.

THE SAMVEDA: The Samaveda is another one of the four Vedas, the ancient scriptures of Hinduism. It is primarily a collection of melodies (saman) used in reciting Vedic hymns. Unlike the Rigveda, which consists mainly of hymns in praise of various deities, the Samaveda focuses on the musical aspects of these hymns and their proper chanting during Vedic rituals. Key features of the Samaveda include melodies and hymns that are sung rather than recited straightforwardly. The melodies are considered crucial because they are believed to profoundly affect the mind and spirit of both the performer and the listener. Many of the verses in the Samaveda are taken directly from the Rigveda, but they are rearranged and set to musical notes and patterns. Thus, while the words are the same as in the Rigveda, their presentation and use differ significantly. The Samaveda is divided into three main parts: the Archika or Purvarchika, the Uttararchika, and the Uha Archika. These parts correspond to the different stages of a typical Vedic ritual and include specific chants and melodies for each. The priests who specialized in chanting and reciting the Samaveda were known as Udgatri. Their role was crucial in performing sacrificial rituals and invoking the divine through the power of the Samavedic melodies. The Samaveda, along with the Rigveda, Yajurveda, and Atharvaveda, forms an integral part of Vedic literature and has been preserved through oral tradition and later written texts. It is valued not only for its religious and ritualistic significance but also for its musical and poetic elements, reflecting ancient India's cultural and spiritual practices.

THE YAJURVEDA: The Yajurveda is one of the four Vedas, Hinduism's ancient and sacred scriptures. It primarily consists of prose mantras (Yajus) and verses (richas) used by priests during Vedic rituals and ceremonies. The word "Yajur" means "prose formula" or "ritual formula," indicating its role in providing the procedural steps and prayers used by priests in performing rituals. The Yajurveda is traditionally divided into two main branches or versions: Shukla Yajurveda, also known as the "White Yajurveda," contains the original verses along with their explanations and rituals. Krishna Yajurveda, the "Black Yajurveda," consists mainly of the mantras (verses) without detailed explanations. According to Vedic tradition, the Yajurveda serves as a guidebook for priests (acharya) who perform rituals and sacrifices (yajna). It provides precise instructions on conducting these rituals, including the specific mantras to be chanted, the sequence of actions, and the offerings to be made to various deities. The Yajurveda contains a collection of hymns and verses dedicated to multiple gods and goddesses, such as Agni (the god of fire), Indra (the king of gods), Soma (the god associated with the sacred drink of the same name), and others. These hymns are meant to invoke divine blessings and ensure the successful completion of rituals. Apart from its ritualistic importance, the Yajurveda also contains philosophical teachings and insights into cosmology, ethics, and the nature of reality. It reflects ancient Vedic society's worldview and spiritual practices, providing a foundation for Hindu religious thought and practice. Like other Vedas, the Yajurveda was initially transmitted orally through generations of priests and scholars before being compiled and recorded in written form. Its preservation has been meticulous, ensuring that its rituals and knowledge have been passed down through millennia. In summary, the Yajurveda plays a crucial role in Hinduism as a repository of ritual knowledge and spiritual wisdom, guiding practitioners in performing sacred ceremonies and offering insights into ancient Indian culture and philosophy.

THE ATHARVAVEDA: The Atharvaveda is one of the four Vedas, the ancient sacred texts of Hinduism. It differs from the other three Vedas (Rigveda, Samaveda, and Yajurveda) in content, style, and purpose. Critical aspects of the Atharvaveda include a diverse collection of hymns, spells, charms, and incantations. These texts cover many subjects, including healing, magic, astrology, rituals for domestic life, and prayers for prosperity and protection. The Atharvaveda is believed to have been composed over a longer time than the other Vedas. Its hymns are attributed to sages or rishis such as Atharvan and Angiras. The Atharvaveda is divided into 20 books or sections (kandas), each dealing with different aspects of life, rituals, and philosophical concepts. Some topics covered include health and disease, rites of passage (such as marriage and funerals), agriculture, governance, and spiritual knowledge. Like the other Vedas, the Atharvaveda contains mantras (verses) used in rituals and ceremonies. However, its emphasis on practical aspects of life, such as healing and protection from evil, distinguishes it from the more purely ritualistic focus of the Rigveda and Yajurveda. Alongside its practical teachings, the Atharvaveda also contains philosophical discussions on the nature of existence, the soul, and ethics. It offers insights into the moral and ethical principles that guided ancient Indian society. Like the other Vedas, the Atharvaveda has been preserved through an oral tradition for centuries before being recorded in written form. Its teachings continue to influence Hindu religious practices, particularly in healing, protection, and domestic life rituals. In summary, the Atharvaveda is a significant Vedic text that provides a comprehensive view of ancient Indian culture, spirituality, and practical wisdom. It complements the other Vedas by offering insights into everyday concerns and applying spiritual knowledge in daily life. Each Veda consists of various texts and layers.

SAMAHITAS: Samhitas are the core texts containing hymns and verses.

BRAHMANAS: They are the prose texts that explain the rituals and ceremonies described in the Samhitas.

ARANYAKAS: Aranyakas are Texts that provide philosophical interpretations and are intended for rituals performed in seclusion (in the forest).

UPANISHADS: The Upanishads, also known as Vedanta, are philosophical texts that explore the deeper meaning of rituals and hymns, focusing on spiritual knowledge and the nature of reality. In summary, the Vedas encompass hymns, rituals, chants, philosophical insights, and spiritual wisdom. They are considered sacred scriptures in Hinduism and are foundational to its religious and intellectual traditions.

CHAPTER 3
THE MAHAJANAPADAS

Mahajanapadas_(c._500_BCE)

The Kuru Kingdom was formed between 1000 and 800 BCE, and it is the first known center of power in the Indian subcontinent, with Hastinapur as its capital (at least for most of the kingdom's existence). The kingdom had a central control and jurisdiction based in the capital, divided into regions and districts. Kuru region was a region in the Kuru Kingdom inhabited by most of the kingdom's subjects, and it was further divided into provinces, regions, and territories. Kurujangala was another region in the kingdom, mostly covered in thick jungle. It was the home to the Jangala tribe, whose survival greatly depended on the flow of the Yamuna. Kurujangala was further split into three regions, one of which had three cities: Panaprashta, Swarnprastha, and Indraprastha. According to literature sources, after the Middle Vedic period, the Kuru Kingdom's first capital was Indraprastha. However, scholars claim that the first capital was Asandivat in Haryana. The kingdom mainly comprised nomadic tribes and tribes that relied on domestic animals. These tribes descended from the mountains before the Battle of the Ten Kings, shifting toward the Ganges plains. Pastoral and nomadic tribes shifted to agriculture, cultivating barley and rice.

The kingdom of Panchala grew to be one of the strongest kingdoms in ancient India, lasting between 900 BCE and 500 BCE. Panchala was located in Doab, a land region between the Ganges and the Yamuna. Panchala had strong diplomatic relations with the Kuru Kingdom and emerged as a power center to the east of the Kuru Kingdom. According to scholars, Panchala was formed from multiple tribes, including the Krivi tribe, which might have come to this region from the Indus River plains.

By the end of 500 BCE, Panchala had ceased to exist as a kingdom and had transformed into an oligarchy as part of the Solasa (Sixteen) Mahajanapadas.

Mahajanapadas, also known in the written form as the Maha Janapadas, is translated as the "great country" in Sanskrit, which partly explains their political and cultural significance in ancient India. Initially, the Mahajanapadas were perhaps an accidental alliance and union between various tribal states and kingdoms that emerged in the plains of the Ganges and Indus. Over time, they became a significant political body with multiple independent authorities. The Mahajanapadas were formed around 550 BCE, coinciding with the Kuru Kingdom's deterioration, taken over by the Salva tribe. The kingdoms that formed the Mahajanapadas were less invasive than the Salva, as these kingdoms expanded politically and territorially by taking land and raiding.

State polities and societies emerged in the 6th/5th century BCE in a belt stretching from Gandhara in the northwest to Anga in eastern India, extending into the Malwa region. Assaka (Ashmaka) in the upper Godavari valley in lists of the great states of the time suggests that similar processes were also underway in parts of trans-Vindhyan India. Buddhist and Jaina texts list 16 powerful states (solasa-mahajanapada) that flourished in the early 6th century BCE. (Janapada also meant a region consisting of urban and rural settlements and its inhabitants.) Apart from these, there must have been smaller states, chiefdoms, and tribal principalities.

In the later Vedic period, agriculture and iron helped people settle down at a particular place. From the 6th century BCE onwards, the outlines of the political histories of North India become more explicit, and the kings and religious figures mentioned in many literary traditions can be identified as factual and historical, unlike the earlier parts of the epic-Purana genealogy that seemed to be mythical. The permanent settlements led to the foundation of Janapadas, or small territorial states under the control of a king. The main area of political activity gradually shifted from Western UP to Eastern UP and Bihar. This region was fertile due to the river systems and rainfall and was closer to iron production centers. Better iron tools and weapons made some territorial states very large. They came to be called as Mahajanapadas. Most of the Mahajanapadas were situated north of the Vindhyas, between Bihar in the east and the subcontinent's northwest frontier. The list of these Mahajanapadas (sixteen) with their capitals is given below:

1. Anga   Capital: Champa
2. Magadh   Capital: Rajagir
3. Kasi   Capital: Kasi
4. Vatsa   Capital: Kausambi
5. Kosala   Capital: Sravasti
6. Saurasena   Capital: Mathura
7. Panchala   Capital: Kampilya
8. Kuru   Capital: Indraprastha
9. Matsya   Capital: Viratnagar
10. Chedi   Capital: Banda
11. Avanti   Capital: Ujjain
12. Gandhar   Capital: Taxila
13. Kamboj   Capital: Pooncha
14. Asmaka   Capital: Paithan
15. Vajji   Capital: Vaishali
16. Malla   Capital: Kusinara

Champa was one of the main cities in ancient India, located in the present-day region of western Bengal and Bihar. Anga became one of the sixteen oligarchic republics in the second wave of urbanization that shifted from the Indus to the Ganges. Anga was an important trading center in ancient India, as was Assaka, located in present-day Maharashtra in central India. One of the kingdoms that later became a part of the Mauryan Empire was Avanti. It was one of the spiritual centers of Buddhism and was divided into two provinces with a natural border in the form of the river Vetravati (Betwa). The Chedi clan was one of the oldest in ancient India. It is mentioned in the old scriptures of the Rig Veda and was divided into two different settlements. One of the settlements was located near the Yamuna River, and the other bloomed in the mountains of Nepal. The Gandhara had existed as a tribe since the beginning of the Vedic period. The Gandhara were known for being somewhat aggressive and very familiar with warfare. The Kamboja tribe, which later became one of the sixteen Mahajanapadas, was mentioned as early as the Gandhara, as they were set on both sides of the Hindu Kush. Kamboja was an Indo-Iranian tribe that came to the region in the first wave of urbanization. The Kashi settled around Varanasi, which got its name from the two rivers surrounding it, the Varuna and Assi. Kashi was the most powerful kingdom of all the Mahajanapadas until the emergence of Buddhism. Kosala was located near the river Ganges from the south and surrounded by the Himalayas in the north. In contrast, another river, the Gandaki, marked the natural border of the kingdom in the east. Kashi merged with Kosala after the rise of Buddhism in the 5th century BCE and was later part of the Mauryan Empire. In the 5th century BCE, Kuru became a republic and one of the Mahajanapadas after the Salva invasion. Matsya once belonged to the kingdom of Chedi. Matsya eventually gained its autonomy and became one of the sixteen prominent kingdoms in ancient India, taking the territory of Jaipur, Bharatpur, and Alwar. Magadha emerged as a strong but loathed kingdom in present-day Bihar. This was because Magadhas weren't Brahmins. Despite its ill-disposed status among other Brahmin kingdoms, Magadha was still one of the strongest kingdoms in ancient India. Malla is often mentioned in the Buddhist scriptures, as Buddha spent his last day in one of the nine provinces of Malla, where he also had his last meal. Malla is also described as one of the strongest tribes in India.

The Panchalas settled east from the Kuru tribe between the Ganges and the Himalayas. Panchala was initially a monarchy and relied on the rule of a king; however, it later transformed into a republic in the 5th century BCE with the coalition of the sixteen oligarchic republics. Surasena was one of the chief kingdoms during the rise of Buddhism. One of the kings of Surasena, Avantiputra, was also one of Buddha's main disciples, and he promoted the sacred knowledge of Buddhism throughout the kingdom. In the deep north of ancient India was Vajji or Vriji, one of the most influential kingdoms among the Mahajanapadas around the 5th century BCE. Vajji consisted of nine different tribes, an important center of Buddhism. It helped spread Buddha's doctrine and spiritual philosophy. Vamsa, or Vatsa, is an offspring republic derived from the Kurus. It occupied the territory around present-day Allahabad in Uttar Pradesh. Its richest and most powerful city was the capital of Kaushambi. Kaushambi was one of the main power centers in the region, with numerous merchants residing there. The capital grew to be prosperous thanks to the fact that it was a natural strategic center of imported and exported goods and a favorite stop of travelers coming from the south and northwest. Udayana was the king of Vamsa during the time of Buddha. He was a powerful ruler and one of Buddha's followers. Udayana promoted Buddhism and made it the main religion of his kingdom.

Monarchy-oriented states were centered in the plains of the Ganges. Kings enjoyed the highest status, and the monarchy was hereditary. Usually, kings were Kshatriyas, who were aggressive in nature and performed Ashvamedha and Rajasuya sacrifices. Gana sanghas, or republics, were established in the northwest provinces, foothills of the Himalayas, and less fertile regions. Panini, Kautilya, Mahabharata, Pali, and Greek texts mentioned Gana sanghas or republics. There were ten republics, according to Buddhist literature. They were Mallas of Kushinagar, Mallas of Pava, Shakyas of Kapilavasthu, Kolyas of Ramagama, Moriyas of Pipalivana, Bullyas of Alakappa, Kalamarad of Kesapatta, Baggas of Samasmagiri: Lichchavi of Vaishali, and Videha of Mithila. Shakyas, Kolyas, Lichavi, Malla, and Moriya are potent republics. These republics included Shakyas, Kolyas, Mallas, Vajji, and Yadava groups. Aryans, who believed in freedom, established these republics. They opposed monarchy, traveled toward the foothills of the Himalayas, and started republics. Ganathanthras continued the traditions of Aryan factions, but later, they gave up a democratic monarchy. They started administration through representative committees. The head of the family was a member of the representative committee. The president of the committee was called the King. King was the republic's leader, and his position was not hereditary. If a decision could not be taken by consensus, voting was followed. Individual opinion was given prominence. The great religious thinker of the 6th century B.C. Gautama Buddha belonged to the Shakya clan. The rule of high caste and wealth was more prominent in the republics. They played a significant role in the decisions of representative committees; small republics could not fight with Vatsa, Kosala, Avanti, and Magadha and lost their significance. Later, they bent towards monarchy and blamed it for their decline.

The untimely political fight among these Mahajanapadas led to one of them, Magadha, emerging as the most powerful state and the center of a vast empire.

CHAPTER 4
BUDDHISM

INTRODUCTION

Gautam Buddha was born around the 6th century BCE into a noble family in ancient India in the region that is now Nepal.

Gautama Buddha's childhood name was Siddhartha. He was born as a royal prince in 563 B.C., in Lumbini, near Kapilavasthu, on the foothills of Nepal. His father, Shuddodana, belonged to Shakya, the Kshatriya clan of Kapilavasthu. He was the elected king of Kapilavasthu and the leader of the Shakya Republic. Siddhartha's mother, Mayadevi, belonged to the royal family of Kosala. She died when Siddhartha was just a seven-day-old baby. Mayadevi's sister, Prajapathi Gautami, looked after him. A Brahmin sage visited Shuddodana to predict Siddhartha's fortune. The Sage examined the child and told the king that the boy could become a Chakravarthi, a ruler of the entire world, or an ascetic.

Suddhodana did not want his son to turn his back on the world, so he took great pains to shield him from its sorrows, raising him in a highly artificial atmosphere surrounded by luxury and pleasant things. Shuddodana shifted his son from the unpleasant relations of daily life.

Years after this, at sixteen years of age, Siddhartha married Yashodrara, the prince of the Koliya Republic.

They had a son, Rahula. Siddhartha's early life was marked by privilege and luxury. He was raised in opulence, shielded from the world's harsh realities. However, his upbringing did not protect him from the questions that existed and arose in the face of human suffering worldwide, which Siddhartha was deeply troubled by. Siddhartha once ventured outside the palace with his charioteer, Chandak. There, he discovered the suffering of his people, which had a significant impact on him. On his tour of the city, he saw four sights, which were: 1. A sick man 2. An old man 3. A dead body 4. An ascetic. The first three scenes brought home to him the harsh realities and inevitabilities of old age, sickness, and death, while the fourth pointed to how to deal with these inevitabilities.

Motivated by a profound sense of compassion and a burning desire to understand the nature of existence, Siddhartha embarked on a spiritual quest. Siddhartha left his home and family and wandered around for six years, seeking the truth.

At 29, he renounced his princely life, leaving behind his family, wealth, and all worldly attachments. This act was a radical departure from societal expectations, as he sought a more profound truth beyond the confines of material wealth and social status. Siddhartha immersed himself in the ascetic practices prevalent in ancient India for six years. He sought out renowned spiritual teachers and engaged in rigorous self-mortification, believing that extreme renunciation of worldly pleasures would lead to enlightenment. However, he soon realized that these extreme practices did not provide his sought answers. Despite subjecting himself to severe physical challenges, he found himself no closer to understanding the nature of suffering and how to stop it. Realizing his limitations, Siddhartha abandoned these practices and adopted a middle way, a balanced approach between self-indulgence and self-mortification. The historical context and early life of Siddhartha Gautama provide a backdrop for understanding the transformative journey he undertook. His decision to give up his privileged life and seek answers was a radical departure from societal norms. It reflects the universal human quest for meaning and understanding in the face of life's complex challenges. Siddhartha's journey serves as an inspiration to seekers of truth and wisdom. It reminds us that enlightenment is not limited to a specific background or circumstance. It resonates with our yearning for deeper understanding and liberation from suffering.

He attached himself to teachers but was not satisfied by their teachings. Accompanied by five wandering ascetics, he practiced severe austerities until his body was skinny and weak. He then realized that he must nourish his body and try to attain peace of mind. His companions abandoned him, thinking he had compromised his asceticism. A young woman named Sujata offered him a bowl of milk- rice. Nourished with food, he sat under the pipal tree again, resolving not to get up until he attained enlightenment. Some texts describe his rising to progressively higher and higher states of knowledge through meditation. Others describe how a wicked being, Mara, tried to tempt and taunt him out of his meditative state, all in vain. Siddhartha ultimately attained enlightenment and became known as BUDDHA., the enlightened one.

The fundamental teachings of the Buddha form a vital quality and feature of Buddhism. They offer profound insights into the nature of existence, the causes of suffering, and the path to liberation. These teachings, known as the Dharma, provide a comprehensive framework for understanding and transcending suffering.

The Buddha addressed his teaching to the monastic order and the other followers. The core of his doctrine is expressed in the Aria-Sachchani (Four Noble Truths): there is suffering (dukkha); it has a cause (samudaya); it can be removed (nirodha), and the way to achieve this is by following the Atthanga-magga (Eight-fold Path). This path consists of several interconnected activities related to knowledge, conduct, and meditative practices. It comprises the correct view, intention, speech, action, livelihood, effort, mindfulness, and concentration. Meditation is crucial in Buddhism and key to achieving mental calm and insight. However, a detailed treatment of meditative techniques appears in later Buddhist texts. The path taught by the Buddha is often referred to as the Middle Path—one between extreme indulgence and extreme asceticism. Dukkha and its extinction are central to the Buddha's doctrine. The Buddha taught that everything is suffering (sabbat dukkha). This can be seen as an extraordinarily pessimistic or an extremely realistic teaching. Suffering refers not only to the actual pain and sorrow experienced by an individual but also to the potential to experience these things. States of happiness or pleasure are unstable and temporary, as they depend on the senses' gratification through particular objects or experiences. The reasons for suffering include human propensities such as desire, attachment, greed, pride, aversion, and ignorance. Desire (Trishna) is central to the cause and removal of suffering. All this is connected with another aspect of existence emphasized in the Buddha's teaching—impermanence (anichcha). Impermanence has many facets. Concerning an individual's life, no being or power in the universe can prevent old age, sickness, and death. At a more fundamental level, what we consider the 'I' or 'me' is an ever-changing compound of a succession of experiences and consciousness.

THE FOUR NOBLE TRUTHS IN BRIEF:

Tapa Shotor Seated Buddha

The Four Noble Truths serve as the foundation of the Buddha's teachings. They acknowledge the existence of suffering (dukkha) as an inherent part of human existence. The First Noble Truth recognizes the reality of suffering in various forms, including physical pain, emotional distress, and the unsatisfactory nature of worldly experiences. The Second Noble Truth delves into the causes of suffering, highlighting the role of craving and attachment. It teaches that our desires and attachments to transient things and experiences lead to suffering. The Third Noble Truth offers hope by proclaiming that the end of suffering is attainable. It emphasizes that a lack of craving and attachment makes liberation from suffering possible. The Fourth Noble Truth outlines the Eightfold Path, which provides a practical guide for overcoming suffering and gaining freedom.

THE EIGHTFOLD PATH IN BRIEF:

The Eightfold Path is the path to liberation and enlightenment. It encompasses eight interconnected aspects: Right Understanding, Right Intention, Right Speech, Right Action, Right Livelihood, Right Effort, Right Mindfulness, and Right Concentration. Each element represents a key component of ethical conduct, mental discipline, and wisdom. Proper Understanding involves developing a deep understanding of the Four Noble Truths and the nature of reality. Right Intention involves wholesome intentions and moving away from harmful desires. Right Speech emphasizes truthful, kind, and beneficial communication. Right Action encourages ethical behavior and refraining from harming others. Right Livelihood involves living morally and supporting the path of awakening. Right Effort emphasizes the development of wholesome qualities and the abandonment of unwholesome ones. Right Mindfulness involves developing present-moment awareness and mindfulness in all activities. Right Concentration involves focused and concentrated states of mind through meditation. The sacred texts of Buddhism hold immense significance as they contain the teachings and wisdom of the Buddha and his disciples. These texts guide and provide insights into the nature of existence, the path to liberation, and the cultivation of knowledge.

Wheel of Existence

Buddha spread Buddhism in Magadha and the neighboring state, Varanasi. Rajagruha, Shravasthi, Vaishali, and Nalanda were the cities he visited. Emperors, kings, women, the poor, and many people followed him. Bimbisara, emperor of Magadha, and his son Ajathashathru became his disciples. When he visited Kapilavasthu, his father Shuddodana, his wife Yashodrara, and son Rahula became his disciples. For forty-five years, he preached Buddhism, and in 483 B.C., in Kushinagar of Malla Republic, at the age of eighty, he attained Nirvana. It happened on a full moon day of Vaisakha month. Buddha's birth, enlightenment, and death occurred on a full moon day in Vaisakha. Therefore, the day is celebrated as Buddha Purnima.

Buddha advocated complete renunciation of the desire for happiness. He advocated an eight-fold path for mental peace, freedom, and enlightenment. Buddhism did not believe in the concept of the soul. It proclaimed an eight-fold path for the improvement of moral and religious life. Buddha said salvation is possible without the intervention of priests. The eightfold path is also known as the middle path. It is a practice of non-extremism. It is a balanced state between worldly pleasure and extreme self-mortification. Buddhism did not believe in any God and ritualistic sacrifices and did not force celibacy and non-violence on any individual. Buddha believed in the equality of all. Buddha created certain principles or ethical values for his disciples. They were: 1. Non acquisition of others property. 2. Non-violence. 3. Non-use of liquor. 4. Non corruption. 5. Truthfulness. Buddha neither accepted nor rejected the existence of God in his teachings. He opposed all forms of violence, the caste system, animal sacrifice, the study of Vedas, and the sanctity of the Sanskrit language. Buddha gave importance to Karma and the rebirth principle. He believed Karma was the reason for rebirth. According to him, Karma is caught in the chains of intent and consequence. All actions are intended, and they have their consequences. Buddha advocated Nirvana as the only way of releasing oneself from this chain.

Though Buddha did not mention anything about God, he disagreed with idol worship. But in the later years, Buddha was worshipped as an idol by his disciples. The familiar people liked Buddhism as it did not fall prey to philosophical controversies. It did not accept the caste system, which in turn attracted a vast number of low-caste people. Women were also encouraged to join 'Buddhism.' Buddhist democratic and simple principles attracted many people to its fold. Buddhism attracted more people who lived in complex regions. They got converted to Buddhism. The traditional Brahmins ill-treated the people of Magadha, which made many people join Buddhism. Buddha's personality and his teaching helped in the spread of Buddhism. Buddha preached in the common language of people, Pali, which helped his principle reach ordinary people. He organized Buddhist monasteries and allowed people irrespective of their caste and gender. Magadha, Kosala Kausambi, and many other republics became followers of Buddhism. Many years after the death of Buddha, Ashoka, the Mauryan emperor, accepted Buddhism. He spread Buddhism to Central Asia, West Asia, and Sri Lanka. During his reign, Buddhism became an international religion. Today, Buddhism is a prominent religion in Sri Lanka, Burma, Tibet, Japan, and China. Many became his followers. His followers are divided into two classes. One class was ascetics called Bhikshu (monks), and the other was Upasaka and Upasaki, who remained in their material life but followed Buddhism.

The Bhikshu (monks) were Dharma Pracharakas (Missionaries). Buddhism set some principles for them to follow. Sangha (Monasteries) of female Bhikshu (Bhikshuni) was also started under the influence of Prajapathi Gauthami (Stepmother of Buddha) and Ananda (Buddha's disciple). There were many restrictions to joining Buddhism. Physically challenged patients with infectious deceases, criminals, and debtors were forbidden from joining Buddhist monasteries. Bhikshus had to follow strict rules regarding discipline, food, and dress. The monasteries had internal administration on the lines of republics administered by Sangha Parinayaka. Buddhist ascetics had to follow specific rules, some of them being truthfulness, not stealing, celibacy, nonviolence, not taking liquor, non-indulgence in dancing and singing, avoiding associations with women, no use of flowers or perfumes, not taking food at forbidden times, not sleeping in a comfortable bed, etc. Those interested in joining Buddhist monasteries had to accept Buddha as their religious Guru and follow five ethical values. Four days a month, it must be celebrated as sacred, and it is called Uposatva in India and Roya in Srilanka. Celebrating Vaisakha Poornima or Buddha Poornima was made compulsory.

BUDDHIST COUNCILS:

Buddhist Ordination Ceremony

Buddhist councils are gatherings of monastic communities formed to address and resolve doctrinal and disciplinary disputes. The sanghas conduct these councils periodically.

The first Buddhist council occurred in 487 B.C. in Rajgir (formerly Rajgriha). It was presided over by Mahakassapa and sponsored by Ajatashatru, the king of Magadha. The primary aim of this council was to codify Buddhist teachings, resulting in the compilation of the Vinaya and Sutta Pitaka.

The second Buddhist council was convened in 387 B.C. at Vaishali, approximately a hundred years after the Buddha's Maha Parinirvana. This council was organized by Kalasoka, the Magadhan king, to address the differences between liberal and fundamentalist Buddhists. It was presided over by Sabakami.

The third Buddhist council was held in 251 B.C. at Pataliputra, under the patronage of Emperor Ashoka. Moggaliputta Tissa presided over it and focused on codifying the Abhidhamma Pitaka.

The fourth Buddhist council convened in 102 A.D. at Kundalavana in Kashmir, under the patronage of King Kanishka of the Kushan dynasty. Ashvaghosha and Vasumitra presided over this council, which produced the Mahavibhasa and Upadesha commentaries on the Tripitakas. The council debated using Sanskrit instead of Pali and witnessed a schism in Buddhism.

Nalanda

A hundred years after the Buddha's Maha Parinirvana, the second Buddhist council divided Buddhism into two schools: Sthaviravada and Mahasanghika. The Fourth Buddhist Council later divided Buddhism into two major sects: Hinayana and Mahayana. In the 8th century A.D., a new sect called Vajrayana emerged in Buddhism, which included hymns and goddess worship (notably Tara). Vajrayana is often divided into two parts: the right and the left.

HINAYANA AND MAHAYANA:

Hinayana was a traditional sect, whereas Mahayana was a liberal one. Hinayana believed in individual salvation, whereas Mahayana aimed at universal salvation. Hinayana followers believed in the basic principles of Buddha, whereas Mahayana believed in the teaching of Bodhisattva. Hinayans worshipped symbols, and Mahayanas worshipped Buddhist statues. Hinayana followers used Pali in their texts, but Mahayanas used Sanskrit.

CONTRIBUTION OF BUDDHISM TO INDIAN CULTURE:

Buddhism emerged as a transformative religious framework in India, offering a compelling alternative to the entrenched practices of Vedic religion. The teachings of Siddhartha Gautama, known as the Buddha, emphasized simplicity and mindfulness, attracting a diverse array of followers who found solace in its rejection of the rigid Varna (caste) system that characterized contemporary society.

Central to the evolution of Buddhism was the introduction of idol worship, particularly prominent within the Mahayana tradition, where followers revered the Buddha as a divine figure. This shift significantly influenced Hindu worship practices, leading to an increased embrace of idol veneration across various sects.

The rise of Buddhism also catalyzed the establishment of several prestigious centers of learning, such as the renowned universities of Nalanda, Vikramasheela, Valabhi, and Taxila. These institutions became intellectual beacons, drawing scholars from across Asia. The spread of Buddhism was further bolstered by the patronage of influential rulers like Ashoka, Kanishka, and Harsha, who supported the faith within their territories and facilitated its diffusion into neighboring countries.

Moreover, Buddhism played a crucial role in shaping the ethical frameworks of these monarchs, fostering a culture of peace and nonviolence. Ashoka, remarkably, became a symbol of this philosophy after the harrowing battle at Kalinga in 261 B.C., which led him to renounce violence and embrace the principles of compassion and tolerance.

Buddhism's literary contributions were significant as well, enriching both Pali and Sanskrit literature. Important texts such as the Vinaya, Sutra, and Abhidhamma Pitaka were composed in Pali, while illustrious works like the Deepavamsha and Mahavamsa also emerged during this period. The Mahayana sect notably emphasized the use of Sanskrit, with scholars like Ashwaghosha creating significant literary masterpieces such as the "Buddhacharita."

In terms of artistic expression, Buddhism left an indelible mark on Indian art and architecture. The construction of stupas, viharas (monasteries), chaityas (prayer halls), and intricately carved pillars showcased the architectural ingenuity of the time. Notable examples of this architectural legacy include the Sanchi Stupa and the awe-inspiring cave temples located in Karle and Nasik, as well as the Buddha Stupa in Amaravati.

Additionally, the exquisite cave paintings in Ajanta and Ceylon highlight the unique artistic contributions of Buddhism, characterized by their vivid storytelling and intricate details. Under the influence of Greek culture, the Kushan Empire saw the rise of Gandhara art, which produced stunning statues of the Buddha, further enriching the visual landscape of Buddhism in India.

DECLINE OF BUDDHISM:

The decline of Buddhism unfolded with a surprising rapidity, paralleling its earlier expansion. While the teachings of Buddhism gained traction across Central and East Asia, this growth could not prevent its diminishment in its place of origin, India. Several intertwined factors contributed to this significant decline, attributed to theological, social, and political dimensions.

Initially, the simplicity and accessibility of Buddha's teachings, coupled with the use of Pali—a widely spoken language among the populace—played a pivotal role in attracting a diverse following. This grassroots enthusiasm, however, saw a marked transformation following the Maha Parinirvana of Buddha. After his passing, the once-unified movement began to diversify significantly, resulting in the emergence of various sects, notably Hinayana and Mahayana. This fragmentation diluted Buddhism's core principles, creating divisions detrimental to its cohesion and public appeal.

The transition from Pali to Sanskrit marked another turning point for Buddhism. While Sanskrit allowed for more elaborate theological discourse, the shift also fostered the adoption of complex rituals and doctrines, often overshadowing the Buddha's original, straightforward teachings. This transition alienated many grassroots followers who had initially been drawn to the simplicity of Buddhist philosophy, leading to a growing number of adherents who preferred more ornate and, at times, esoteric practices.

Within this complex landscape, the rise of the Vajrayana sect represented yet another layer of divergence. As different interpretations and schools of thought emerged, Buddhism's message became increasingly multifaceted and, unfortunately, muddled. Furthermore, the accumulation of wealth through alms by some Bhikshus—a term for Buddhist monks—led to a troubling trend of materialism. This focus on accumulating wealth rather than on spiritual development fostered a sense of laziness and, in some instances, immoral behavior within monastic communities, tarnishing Buddhism's previously revered reputation.

Another socio-religious factor hindering Buddhism's growth was its treatment of women. During his lifetime, Buddha expressed concerns to his disciple Ananda regarding the challenges of including women in monastic life. This reluctance to fully integrate women into the monastic community may have alienated a significant demographic, limiting the religion's potential for broader acceptance and growth.

Buddhism enjoyed renewed support during the reigns of influential patrons such as Kanishka and Harsha, whose endorsements fostered environments where Buddhist practice and scholarship flourished. However, as the power and influence of these rulers waned, so too did the patronage that Buddhism relied upon for its sustenance. The subsequent revival of Hinduism during the Gupta Empire marked a pivotal moment, as it reinvigorated traditional Indian cultural and religious practices, further marginalizing Buddhism in the process.

The turmoil brought about by the Rajputs, a formidable warrior class in northern India, also contributed to Buddhism's decline. Their frequent clashes with the principles of peace and nonviolence espoused by Buddhism led to increased hostilities. The reign of Pushya Mitra Sunga was particularly harsh for Buddhists; he instituted measures that made life increasingly difficult for those adhering to Buddhist traditions. The invasion of the Huns added a catastrophic layer to the situation. Mihirakula, the king of the Huns, is infamously cited for orchestrating mass killings of Buddhist monks, further decimating the already fragile community. In addition, Shashanka, the king of Gauda, effectively eradicated significant Buddhist infrastructure, having destroyed an estimated 1,500 Buddhist stupas and viharas—temples and monasteries that were crucial for safeguarding the teachings and practices of Buddhism.

Thus, the confluence of these diverse factors—doctrinal fragmentation, socio-political upheaval, material corruption, gender exclusion, and concerted attacks—culminated in a rapid and profound decline of Buddhism in its birthplace, transforming a once-flourishing spiritual tradition into a shadow of its former self.

CHAPTER 5
JAINISM

The term "JAIN" is derived from "JINA," which refers to an individual who has attained complete knowledge and achieved freedom from worldly desires through meditation and nonviolence. Essentially, a "JINA" is a perfect being, and Jains are those who follow the teachings of the JINA. JINAs possess knowledge that can guide others on the path to liberation. Although no JINAs exist today, we can still access their shared teachings.

Being a follower of a JINA means understanding what it means to be a JINA and embodying the qualities that a JINA possesses. It does not involve worshiping statues in hopes of receiving assistance in return. A JINA is a perfect being but is not considered a god and does not have control over your destiny or karma.

A JINA has conquered their senses, passions, and karma. They possess supreme knowledge and perception and are souls free from all attachments and possessions, embodying a true spirit of freedom. Understanding a JINA means finding inspiration in their life and following their way of living.

Jains believe that twenty-four Tirthankaras have advocated for Jainism. The Jain cosmology includes an endless sequence of half-cycles known as "utsarinas" and "avasarpinis," which represent phases of progressive and regressive happiness, respectively. These cycles span vast periods and are divided into six stages called "kalas." Each half-cycle is said to contain 24 Tirthankaras.

In our current half-cycle, known as an avasarpini (a period of regressive happiness), the first Tirthankara is Rishabhadeva. Establishing the historicity of all Tirthankaras presents challenges. Neminatha, the 22nd Tirthankara, is believed to have originated from the Saurashtra region of Gujarat. The 23rd Tirthankara, Parshvanatha, lived in Benaras, while Vardhamana, known as Mahavira (meaning "great hero"), is recognized as the 24th Tirthankara.

Mahaveer, also known as Swami Mahavir, was born in 540 B.C. in Kundagram, Vaishali, in Bihar. His father, Siddhartha, belonged to the Ikshvaku clan and was the leader of the Kshatriya republic of Jnatrika. His mother, Trishala, was a princess of the Lichchavi clan and the sister of King Chetak of the Vaishali republic. (Chetak's daughter married Bimbisara, the king of Magadha.) Consequently, Mahaveer was related to both the Lichchavi and Magadha clans.

Originally named Vardhaman, he received a formal education during his childhood. At the age of eighteen, he married Yashodrara and had a daughter named Priyadarshika. Vardhaman showed an early interest in religion and disapproved of animal sacrifice, corrupt ceremonial practices, and the increasing immorality in society.

He lost his parents at the age of thirty, and under the influence of Parshvanatha, he decided to renounce worldly life. After obtaining permission from his brother Nandivardhana, he left his family and became an ascetic on the Dashami (tenth day) of Krishna Paksha in the month of Margashirsha.

Vardhaman spent the next twelve years practicing severe asceticism, beginning with two years in the ashram of Parshvanatha. He then wandered throughout India for the following ten years, enduring abuse and inhumane treatment from others without complaint. Mahaveer persistently sought true knowledge.

At the age of forty-two, on a Dashami of Shukla Paksha in the month of Vaishakha, near the village of Jrumbika, he attained 'Kevalya Jnan' under a Shali tree. Following this enlightenment, he was called Mahaveer, meaning "great hero," for overcoming bodily pleasures and desires. He also became known as Jina, the conqueror, as he renounced worldly pleasures. Mahaveera, a significant figure in ancient Indian philosophy, united his disciples who had embraced the path of asceticism. He laid out a clear set of principles for them to adhere to in their quest for spiritual growth and enlightenment. Among his followers, those who renounced their familial ties and worldly pleasures were known as Nigrantha, reflecting their commitment to strict asceticism. In contrast, those who chose to remain within their families while still following his teachings were referred to as Shravak (male follower) and Shravaki (female follower), balancing their spiritual aspirations with their domestic responsibilities.

After attaining enlightenment, Mahaveera embarked on a journey across several important regions of ancient India, including Kosala, Anga, Mithila, and Champa. During his travels, he passionately disseminated his messages of non-violence, truth, and the importance of self-discipline, attracting a diverse audience and influencing many individuals from various walks of life.

Among those who acknowledged and respected his teachings were prominent rulers such as Bimbisara and Ajathashatru, the kings of Magadha, as well as Chandapradotya, the king of Avanti. These influential figures recognized the profound impact Mahaveera was having on society and often sought his guidance.

Over the years, Mahaveera's teachings resonated with thousands of people, leading to a robust following of around 14,000 devoted disciples. His emphasis on ethical living and spiritual discipline inspired many individuals to pursue a higher path.

TEACHINGS OF MAHAVEER SWAMI JI AND PRINCIPLES OF JAINISM

The teachings of Mahaveera and Parshvanatha are considered as the principles of Jainism. Mahaveera rejected the supremacy of Vedas, ritual sacrifices, animal sacrifices, and priests. He opposed the caste system and believed that even a low caste could be superior. Mahaveera thought that no God created the world. He believed that the world consists of two categories. Jiva and Ajiva. Jiva is the soul, and Ajiva is the matter. Both Jiva and Ajiva are eternal truths. They are non-subservient to one another. He said Jiva and Ajiva are responsible for all the actions in the world. Jainism emphasizes Karma, life, and salvation. Mahaveera accepted the Karma principle and believed in rebirth. He said for all the sins and problems, the Karma of the previous birth was responsible. He advocated that the primary intention of one's life should be to release the soul from the clutches of the body. He believed the soul to be responsible for life's creation, destruction, pleasure, and pains. Under the influence of Karma, the soul is habituated to seek pleasures in materialistic belonging and possessions. This is the deep-rooted cause of self-centered violent thoughts, deeds, anger, hatred, greed, and other vices. These result in further accumulation of Karma. The ultimate objective of his teaching is how one can attain total freedom from the cycle of birth. Life, pain, misery, and death can be achieved by achieving a permanent, blissful state. This is also known as liberation, nirvana, absolute freedom, or Moksha.

Mahaveera advocated three gems or three ratnas to liberate oneself. 1. Right path (Samyak Shraddha) 2. Right Knowledge (Samyak Jnana) 3. Right Conduct (Samyak Acharana). The main principles of right conduct are
i) Sympathy with nonviolence, 2) Renunciation, 3) Ignorance, 4) Chaste behavior 5) Asceticism.

Jain texts prescribe more straightforward principles that everyone can follow. They are called Panchasheela principles. Parshvanatha advocated the first four, and Mahaveera added the fifth one. They are: 1. Nonviolence (Ahimsa) 2. Truth (Satya) 3. Non-stealing (Astheya) 4. Non-Possession (Aparigriha) 5. Celibacy (Brahmacharya).

Let us study them in brief:

Nonviolence (Ahimsa): Bhagavan Mahaveera taught us that all living beings desire life, not death. Therefore, no one had the right to take away the life of any other being. Thus, the killing of life is the greatest sin. According to Jainism, killing animals is also a great sin; Jainism goes further and says there is life in trees and plants, life in air, water, etc., and all living beings have an equal right to exist. Therefore, we should not kill the lives of the lowest organisms.

Satya (Truth): Speaking the truth requires moral courage. Only those who have conquered greed, fear, anger, jealousy, ego, vulgarity, frivolity, etc., can talk about the truth. Jainism insisted that one should refrain from falsehood and always speak the truth.

Astheya (Non-Stealing): The vow of non-stealing insists that one should be honest and not steal or rob others of their wealth, belongings, etc. Further, one should not take anything which does not belong to him. It does not entitle one to take away anything which may be lying unattended or unclaimed. One should observe this view very strictly and not touch even a worthless thing that does not belong to him.

Aparigraha (Non-acquisition or possession): Jainism teaches that accumulating worldly wealth can lead to unhappiness and increase the likelihood of committing sins, both physically and mentally. Attachment to material possessions can give rise to negative emotions like greed, jealousy, selfishness, ego, hatred, and violence. Such attachments contribute to the cycle of birth and death. Therefore, anyone seeking spiritual liberation should strive to detach themselves from the pleasurable objects associated with all five senses.

Brahmacharya (Celibacy): Brahmacharya, or celibacy, refers to total abstinence from sexual indulgence. It is believed that sexual desires can cloud one's judgment and distract from the pursuit of moksha (liberation), overshadowing virtues and reason during moments of indulgence. While it may seem easy to avoid physical and sexual activities, it is much more challenging to control subtle desires, as one may still think about the pleasures of sex. Specific rules for observing this vow are established and applicable to monks and householders.

After 200 years following Mahavira's Nirvana, Jainism split into two sects: the Shvetambara and the Digambara. The Shvetambara sect, whose members wear white robes, considered themselves followers of Parshvanatha, while the Digambara sect claimed Mahavira as their guru. The Digambara sect advocated for strict principles, including that true monks should be unclothed.

According to the Shvetambara sect, the fundamental Jain principles are codified in fourteen Purva texts. In the 4th century B.C., when the Magadha state faced a famine, Badrabahu and his disciples migrated to Shravanabelagola. During this time, the Mauryan emperor Chandragupta Maurya also traveled with them. Several Jains chose to remain in Magadha under the leadership of Sthula Bhadra. He called for a meeting of Jain followers to take steps to preserve and codify Jain texts. As a result, twelve parts of the Jain texts were codified.

When Badrabahu returned after twelve years, he opposed the different Jain practices that had developed in Magadha. In response, Sthula Bhadra convened a Jain council to consolidate the codification of the twelve Anga (parts), but this council was boycotted by the Jains who had traveled from the South.

CONTRIBUTIONS OF JAINISM TO INDIAN CULTURE :

Jainism has made significant contributions to Indian culture. The principle of non-violence, a key tenet of Jainism, has become a fundamental aspect of Indian ethos. Under the influence of Jainism, the practice of ritual animal sacrifice, prevalent in Vedic traditions, was abolished. Jainism also opposed the caste system and advocated for equality among all individuals. As a result, the influence of Jainism contributed to the decline of the Vedic religion, prompting necessary reforms within it.

One of Jainism's significant teachings is the principle of non-acquisition, which fostered a culture of charity among the people. Jainism also played a crucial role in developing several languages, including Prakrit, Sanskrit, Tamil, and Kannada. Notable figures such as Simhanandi, Kunda Kundacharya, and Pujyapada produced numerous texts in Sanskrit.

The Chalukyan era is the age of Jain poets, with significant literary figures like Ranna, Ponna, Pampa, and Ravikirthi emerging during this time. The acclaimed Tamil literary work "Thirukkural" was authored by the Jain poet Thiruvalluvar, while the "Shivasindhamani" was written by the Jain poet Thirukkuvi. Prominent scholars such as Haribhadra, Akalanka, Siddhasena, Samantabhadra, and Swami Karthikeya contributed to Jain thought and literature.

In mathematics, Mahaveeracharya is a remarkable Jain scholar who authored important texts on geometry and arithmetic. Additionally, Kumudendu wrote "Bhuvalaya" (Sri Bhuvalaya) in the Anka script. Scholars like Sridhar Acharya produced works in astronomy, astrology, and medicine.

Jainism has also significantly influenced art and architecture. The Jains constructed stupas and temples dedicated to Tirthankaras, and their architectural style is evident in regions such as Mathura, Bundelkhand, Madhya Pradesh, Rajasthan, Gujarat, Girnar, Junagadh, and Karnataka. Mathura is home to statues of Mahaveera and Parshvanatha. Jain art can be seen in caves like Hathigumpha, Udayagiri, and Ellora. The Jain tower in Chittoor is another notable example of Jain architecture. One of the most remarkable architectural feats of the Jains is the construction of a 58.8-foot monolithic statue of Bahubali in Shravanabelagola, located in present-day Karnataka.

DECLINE OF JAINISM IN INDIA:

1. LACK OF ROYAL SPONSORSHIP:

Initially, Jainism received strong royal patronage from kings such as Bimbisara, Ajatasatru, Udayin, and

Kharavela. However, this support dwindled over time, as later kings and princess did not uphold the same level of commitment. The fervor and dedication of rulers like Asoka, Kanishka, and Harsha to promote Buddhism overshadowed Jainism. Consequently, the absence of sincere and determined royal support contributed to Jainism's decline.

2. DECLINE IN EFFORTS:

There was also a decrease in the missionary zeal and commitment of Jaina followers. They became less inclined to take on the challenge of spreading Jainism in villages and towns. Although traders and businessmen remained loyal to Jainism, they were often too busy to engage in its promotion.

3. SEVERITY OF JAINISM:

The stringent principles of Jainism worked against it, leading to its decline. Unlike Buddhism's 'middle path,' Jainism emphasized severe penance, meditation, fasting, and restraint, which many found too difficult to maintain. As a result, people grew disillusioned and began to see Jainism as less appealing. Over time, Jainism, once highly regarded, became increasingly isolated from the populace.

4. COMPLEX PHILOSOPHY:

Much of Jaina philosophy was difficult for the general public to comprehend. Many individuals struggled to grasp concepts such as Jeeva, Ajeeva, Pudgala, and Syadbada. The notion that inanimate objects like stones, water, trees, or earth possessed souls was particularly hard for people to accept. This lack of understanding led to a gradual decline in popular faith in Jainism.

5. DIVISION WITHIN JAINISM:

Factionalism among Jains after Mahavira's death contributed to the decline. Some followers advocated strict adherence to Mahavira's teachings, while others sought to moderate the perceived severity of Jainism. This division created rifts within the community, leading to the emergence of two main groups: the 'Digambara,' led by Bhadrabahu, who renounced clothing and engaged in extreme self-punishment and harsh rituals, and the 'Swetambara,' led by Sitalabahu, who wore white cloth. This division weakened Jainism and hindered its growth.

6. RISE OF BUDDHISM:

The spread of Buddhism also impeded the progress of Jainism. Buddhism offered a simpler, more understandable set of beliefs that were accessible to the average person.

7. CHALLENGES FROM HINDUISM:

Hinduism presented further challenges to Jainism's growth. Influential figures like Nimbarka, Ramanuja, and Sankaracharya reinforced Hinduism's foundations. The rise of Vaishnavism, Shaivism, and Shaktism rendered Jainism comparatively insignificant. As a result, Jainism's decline became both inevitable and unavoidable. While Jainism once thrived, its momentum significantly decreased with the rise of Buddhism and Hinduism, creating persistent obstacles to its spread.

CHAPTER 6
ALEXANDER CONQUEST OF INDIA

In 327 BC, Alexander the Great conquered the Persian Empire. He made good connections with the Bactrian people and married Roxana, the daughter of Bactrian nobleman Oxyartes., who served Bessus, the Satrap of Bactria. She later gave birth to his only son and heir. Alexander was the first Greek to venture this far but wanted to go even further. He crossed the Indus Valley and advanced into India, defeating numerous tribes along the way. While advancing into Punjab, he clashed with the army of King Porus at the Battle of Hydaspes. Although Alexander emerged victorious, it was the most costly battle of his entire military career. Impressed by Porus's courage, he made King Porus the satrap of Punjab. His troops had been on the campaign for over 10 years and were unwilling to fight further. Alexander and his army had heard about the mighty Nanda empire and its ferocious armies by this time. Against the Indian troops, they rebelled at the hypnosis. As the news of the mutiny filtered through the air, reaching Alexander's ears like a chilling wind, he found himself plunged into a whirlpool of contemplation. His thoughts swirled with the weight of the chaos enveloping him as he vividly imagined the faces of the people affected by this upheaval. Days of reflection passed, each moment pressing down on him like the heavy cloak of uncertainty wrapped around his shoulders.

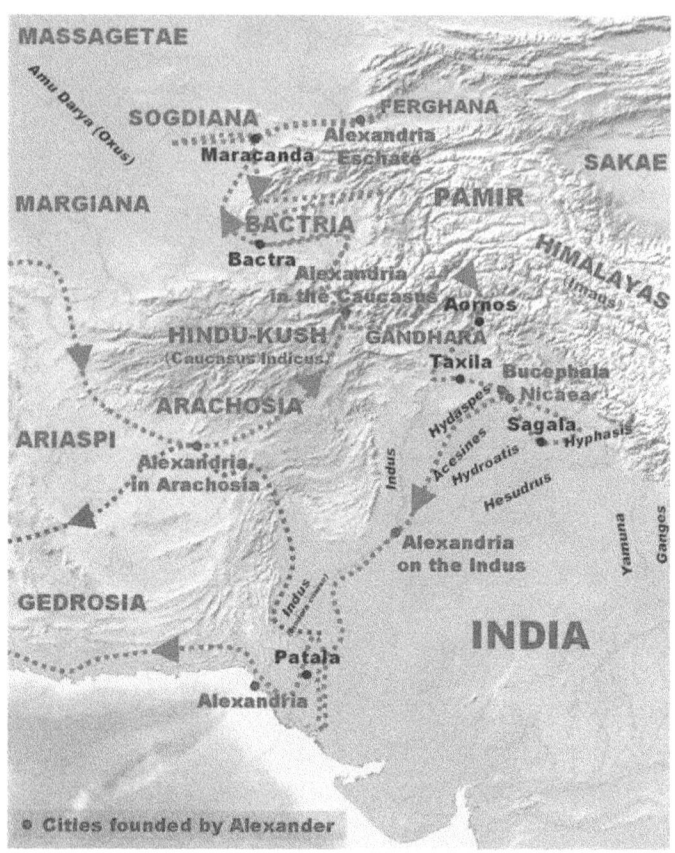

Alexander Conquest Of India

Finally, after wrestling with his emotions and analyzing the precarious situation, he reached a sad conclusion: retreating was the wisest course of action. With a heart burdened by sorrow yet steeled by resolve, he began the long, taxing journey back to his hometown. The landscapes of his childhood beckoned him—rolling hills, whispering trees, and the distant horizon filled with memories—calling him home like a siren's song, promising solace amid the storm. Each step reminded him of the long road ahead, filled with uncertainty and hope intertwined... But on the way, in Opis near modern-day Baghdad, Alexander ordered some of his veterans to return to their homes in Macedon. However, many were angered at perceived insults to their honors and Alexander's adoption of Persian customs, and they rebelled; according to historian Arrian, Alexander executed 13 ringleaders before giving an inspirational speech to his army. His troops begged Alexander for forgiveness, which became one of the most emotional reconciliations between the king and the military. Alexander then started to plan further conquests, but before this could happen, he contracted an unknown illness and died at the age of just 32. On his deathbed, Alexander was the most powerful man in the world. He was asked who his successor would be; his wife Roxana was pregnant then, but she didn't give birth to his son until some months later. So Alexander told them that "to the strongest," meaning his empire would go to the general who could defeat the others in battle. His potential successors, who fought for control of his empire, known as the Diadochi, waged a war for over 50 years. One of his generals, Seleucus 1 Nicator, won much of Alexander's eastern empire and launched his invasion of India.

CHAPTER 7
VISHNUGUPT (CHANAKYA) AND DHANA NAND

Chanakya Artistic Depiction

Vishnugupt was born to a scholarly Brahmin family in the 4th Century BC. He originated from the west coast of the modern-day state of Gujarat and was married to a traditional Brahmin lady. His father's name was Chanak, and his mother's name was Chaneshvari. Vishnugupt was educated but poor, so he headed north to the Nanda empire, seeking opportunity in the prosperous city of Pataliputra (Modern-day Patna). Vishnugupt became a courtly advisor and administrator to King Dhana Nanda.

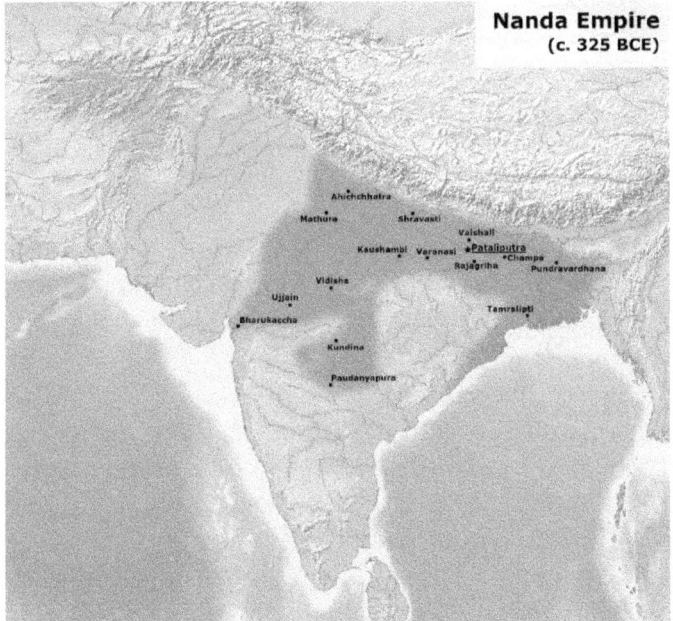

Nanda Empire,_c.325_BCE

In 322 BCE, a new power ascended in the plains of the river Ganges. The same empire that was once too big for Alexander and his army to take on was now under attack. This battle would bring the king of the Nanda Empire, Dhana Nanda, to his knees. According to a legend that draws roots from ancient Indian scriptures, Dhana Nanda, the ruler of the wealthy and vast Nanda Empire, offended Chanakya, a prominent Brahmin, in public. The Buddhist version of the legend says that Chanakya was born with canine teeth, which are considered a sign of royal origin. His mother feared he would abandon her once he became king, so Chanakya broke his teeth to calm his mother. One day, Dhana Nanda organized a ceremony for Brahmins, which Chanakya attended. Once Dhana Nanda saw Chanakya, he was so disgusted and offended by his appearance—with his crooked legs, unsightly face, and broken teeth—that he ordered someone to remove Chanakya from the ceremony. Offended by the king's order, Chanakya promised to end his reign and bring down his empire, which he did with his fosterling, Chandragupta Maurya.

Pandit Vishnugupt (Chanakya) advised Kind Dhana Nanda to form a Nationwide alliance to tackle the incoming foreign aggression. But in his Pride and Arrogance, Dhana Nanda not only ridiculed the scholar but even discredited him. Vishnugupt (Chanakya) was enraged, so he untied his top knot and vowed not to tie it back until the king was dethroned and his supporters uprooted like trees in a storm. Dhana Nanda was then at the peak of his power, and his empire stretched from Punjab to Bengal. His troops were so formidable that Alexander's troops didn't want to go any further into India.

Another potential successor to the throne was Dhana Nanda's son, Pabbata, whom Chanakya convinced to seize the throne. To test who would be a better fit for the Nanda Empire, Chanakya gave an amulet on a thread to both Chandragupta and Pabbata. One night, while Chandragupta was asleep, Chanakya asked Pabbata if he could take off Chandragupta's amulet without cutting the thread or waking him up. After Pabbata failed, Chanakya asked Chandragupta if he could do the same the next night. Chandragupta succeeded, so Chanakya chose him as the next king of the Nanda Empire. There is little historical evidence to confirm any story wrapped in myth and legend, although it is known that Chanakya did help Chandragupta to become a king and the founder of a new empire. Chandragupta was more likely advised and taught by Chanakya, who utilized the power vacuum formed after Alexander the Great's death. Around 323 BCE, Alexander's empire in Asia was divided into regions and pieced into various satraps in the Greater Punjab area, so Chandragupta decided to conquer and subdue Greek satraps in South Asia, knowing that it would pave the way to conquering the Nanda Empire.

There are so many legends surrounding the conquest of the Nanda Empire, but there are few details in Indian scriptures about the end of Nanda or Dhana Nanda that could be true. Most written sources on the conquest of the Nanda Empire were written at least two hundred years after Chandragupta had formed one of the biggest empires in ancient India. Plutarch also wrote about Chandragupta, Nanda's decline, and the Mauryan Empire's rise. As Plutarch writes, young Chandragupta might have met Alexander the Great when he was still a teenager at Taxiles's court, taught by his guru, Chanakya. Maybe Chandragupta saw Alexander as the personification of a universal emperor; after all, he dreamed of becoming one himself, which he later did in his early twenties by forming the Maurya Empire. Many historians argue that Chandragupta might have met Alexander, but there is no factual proof that their encounter ever happened. According to various Latin, Hellenistic, and Indian sources, Chandragupta was determined to bring the Nanda Empire down so he could subdue all of South Asia and establish a firm hold over the Indo-Gangetic Plain. Chandragupta Maurya commenced his conquest by subduing and raiding the surrounding settlements, villages, and regions. Afterward, Chandragupta hired Hindu mercenaries and decided to go for the center of power in the Nanda Empire, targeting the capital of Pataliputra. Chanakya played a crucial role in the conquests of Chandragupta, teaching him everything he knew about politics, forming alliances, conducting wars, and exercising statesmanship. In 323 BC, Chandragupta and Vishnugupta conquered much of the northwest, including Taxila, and set their sights on the Nanda Empire next.

According to legend, after achieving some minor victories on the borders, Chandragupta and Chanakya attempted a direct assault on the Nanda capital of Pataliputra. However, they were defeated and had to retreat while disguised. During their retreat, they overheard a mother scolding her child for getting burned while trying to drink hot soup straight from the center of the bowl. She advised, "Don't be naïve like Chandragupta. Start drinking from the cooler edges first, then work your way to the middle." This conversation prompted Chandragupta and Vishnugupta to realize their mistake: they should have focused on the border territories first, securing small victories before advancing toward the throne of Magadha.

Drawing from the lessons they had learned through their trials, Chandragupta and his allies made their way to the thriving capital of Magadha. A fierce and monumental battle erupted, one that would be remembered in history. The renowned historians Pliny and Plutarch noted the sheer scale of the conflict; the Nanda Empire boasted a formidable army equipped with 200,000 infantry, 80,000 cavalry, 8,000 chariots, and a staggering 6,000 war elephants. In response, Chandragupta assembled an equally vast and determined force, setting the stage for a clash of epic proportions.

The stakes in this battle for control over the Nanda Empire were extraordinarily high, with the very fate of the region hanging in the balance. After a lengthy and arduous struggle, Chandragupta's forces managed to lay siege to the capital of Magadha, ultimately claiming victory. However, the aftermath of the battle is wrapped in historical uncertainty; some accounts suggest that Dhana Nanda, the reigning monarch, met a grim fate at the hands of Vishnugupt, while others propose that he was merely exiled from his throne.

Regardless of the differing narratives surrounding Dhana Nanda's demise, one thing remained clear: Chandragupta emerged victorious and was crowned as the Emperor of Magadha, marking the dawn of the illustrious Mauryan Empire. In the wake of this monumental change in leadership, Vishnugupt—now celebrated for his strategic brilliance—was appointed the chief advisor to the newly crowned Emperor. Over time, he became widely known as Chanakya, a name synonymous with wisdom and guile in the annals of Indian history.

After conquering the Nanda Empire, Chandragupta founded a new empire in 321 BCE while securing the borders to the west and continuing with his expansion politics. In Taxila, Vishnugupt and Chandragupta would change their fortunes and build the foundation of the first great Indian empire, encompassing much of the subcontinent – The Mauryan Empire. While in Taxila, it has been believed that Vishnugupt taught at the prestigious University of Taxila and personally tutored Chandragupta, developing him into a polished, kingly figure, having trained him in politics, military warfare, administration, and much more required to be a Great ruler. He also actively tried to look for allies against Dhana Nanda. Vishnugupt took war loans from the merchant guilds, which was common in India then. Vishnugupt then used the money to hire a group of Greek mercenaries and then struck a deal with a Himalayan King, Parvatika, who would support them with his troops but, in return, would get half of the empire.

One of the greatest legacies of Chanakya, also known as Kautilya in many ancient sources, was the Arthashastra. The Arthashastra is an ancient scripture about politics, statecraft, economy, and military strategy that contains essential lessons and the collected knowledge Chanakya had imparted to Chandragupta. Chandragupta used the Arthashastra to manage and organize his empire, an enormous central power known at this point in India. Chanakya emphasized recruiting spies in the king's name so the ruler would always be aware of what was being discussed among his courtiers, subjects, and neighboring kingdoms. The logistics of running a network of spies are described in the book in detail, including background checks and minister screening.

The book's name, Arthashastra, can be translated as "The Science of Wealth" or "Science of Political Economy." The treatise touches on many subjects, such as the market and trading, economy, law, ethics, and war theories. It explores nature, peace, medicine, animals, agriculture, and diplomacy. The book includes strategies for questions of social welfare, advising the king about actions he should take in case of famine, natural disasters, and other cases of misfortune. For example, if a natural disaster strikes or the empire is affected by famine, the king should absolve those affected from paying taxes. Moreover, the king should start a public project to show the people that their leader was still in control and very potent. Public projects could be building forts, aqueducts, irrigation systems, or similar constructions that would keep chaos or mutiny at bay amidst crises.

After the Maurya Empire was founded, Chanakya naturally became Chandragupta's chief minister. With the help and guidance of Chanakya, Chandragupta captured numerous Indian territories from Greek satraps appointed after Alexander the Great's death. Chandragupta even killed some satraps to show his dominance over the Indo-Gangetic Plain. By 317 BCE, all the Macedonian satraps had been removed from Indian territories or executed by the Mauryan king.

CHAPTER 8
SELEUCUS 1 NIKATOR

Five years later, in 312 BCE, Seleucus I Nicator came on the political scene of ancient India. He threatened Chandragupta's Maurya Empire as his newly founded kingdom faced the empire from its eastern border. Nicator was already familiar with the terrain of the Indian subcontinent, having been one of the generals of Alexander the Great. He was also one of many friends, family members, and generals who fought over the throne of the Alexandrian Empire. A decade after Alexander's death, Nicator formed a new Hellenistic power center called the Seleucid Empire in India. The empire stretched to Mesopotamia and Syria, taking most of Asia Minor and the Iranian Plateau. For a bit of background, Nicator supported Perdiccas after Alexander died in 323 BCE. However, after a mutiny against Perdiccas erupted due to his failure to subdue Ptolemy in Egypt, Nicator conspired with two other generals, Antigenes and Peithon. They killed Perdiccas in 321 BCE. While Antipater (one of Alexander's generals) became the regent of the Macedonian kingdom, Nicator was given the title of Babylonian satrap. However, the shift of power swiftly changed the situation.

Antigonus, perhaps the most powerful Macedonian general at the time, claimed the throne as the new regent, and Nicator didn't have many options but to flee and leave Babylon. Nicator couldn't return to his power center until 312 BCE when he formed his South Asian empire. He gradually took the title of Chiliarch, Shahanshah of Persia, Lord of Asia, and, pretentiously, the King of the Universe. Chandragupta didn't face Nicator directly in a war until 305 BCE. This war is known to history as the Seleucid-Mauryan War. The Hellenistic world and ancient India were clashing yet again. The war would go on for two years, but sadly, details about the Seleucid-Mauryan War are scarce. What is known to history is that Nicator wanted to win over the remaining satraps who once belonged to the Macedonians. At one point during the war, Nicator crossed the river Indus. It is unclear where the war's first battle occurred due to the lack of information, but Seleucus I Nicator faced a wild river with a hostile empire waiting on the other side.

The war ended in 303 BCE with a treaty between the Mauryan Empire and the Seleucid Empire. The treaty was also strengthened with a political marriage. Seleucus gave his daughter's hand, Helena, to Chandragupta, which allowed Helena to become a Mauryan princess. However, the mother of the king's successor wasn't Helena; that honor belonged to Durdhara. Chandragupta had another wife, as polygamy was customary and a part of the monarchial tradition in ancient India. There are no details on the lineage of Durdhara or her life, except for the information that Durdhara gave birth to the heir to the throne, Bindusara. Along with giving his daughter's hand to Chandragupta, Seleucus Nicator also gave up the provinces in the far east of his empire. In return, Chandragupta became his ally and gave him five hundred war elephants, which would help Seleucus in his long war between Alexander's generals and family members fighting over his territories. Chandragupta continued his expansionist politics after 302 BCE, as he now had a valuable ally, keeping the borders between the two empires stable and secure. The Mauryan king extended his empire to the southern parts of India and the Deccan Plateau. When almost the entire Indian subcontinent was unified, Chandragupta and his chief minister Chanakya began reforming politics and the economy.

CHAPTER 9
THE MAURYAN EMPIRE

CHANDRAGUPTA MAURYA
(320 BCE TO 298 BCE)

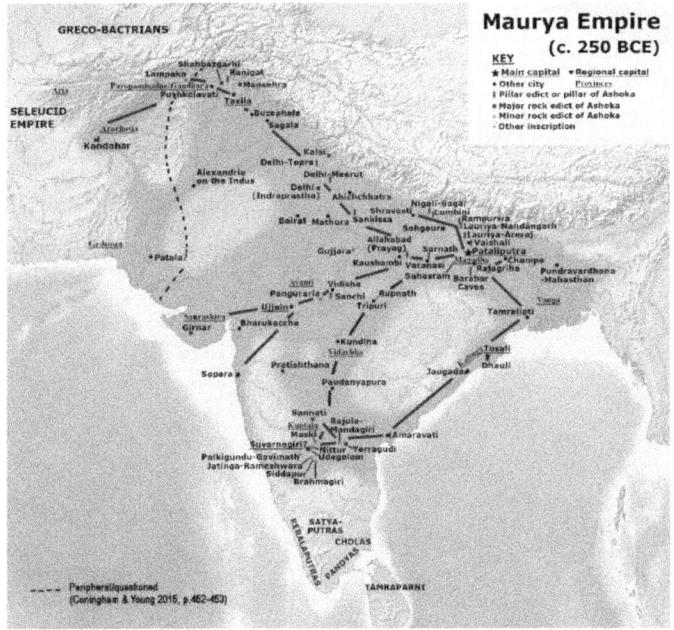

Mauryan Empire 250 BCE to 185 BCE

Chandra Gupta Maurya was the founder of the Mauryan Empire and the first emperor of India. He established a permanent power in the region, liberating the country from the yoke of the Greeks and the tyranny of the Nandas of Magadha. The ancestry of Chandra Gupta Maurya is unclear. A Greek historian, Justin, noted that Chandra Gupta came from a low background. The text Mudra Rakshasa refers to him as "Vrishala" and "Kulahina." Some scholars interpret these terms to mean he was a Shudra and an outcast, while others believe they signify "king of kings" and "of humble birth," respectively.

Mauryan Coin

According to Jain tradition, he was born to the daughter of a village chief known as the Mayura Poshakas. As mentioned in the Vishnu Purana, the Brahmanical tradition states he was born to Mura, a Sudra woman in the court of the Nandas, which led to the surname "Maurya." Some historians suggest he was a member of a powerful Kshatriya tribe called the Moriyas, who were prominent during the time of Buddha. Eventually, the Nandas conquered their territory, leading to the impoverishment of Chandragupta's family. Nonetheless, he held a high position in the Nanda army.

Dhana Nanda, the Nanda king, grew jealous of him and plotted to have him murdered, prompting Chandra

Gupta to flee. After leaving the Nanda kingdom, he resolved to destroy it but lacked the means and wandered for a time. Eventually, he met a learned man named Chanakya, also known as Kautilya, who assisted him in overthrowing the Nanda dynasty. After being insulted by the Nanda king, Chanakya vowed to eradicate the Nanda dynasty. These two great men, united by a common goal, began to gather the resources and army necessary to fulfill their aims.

Chandragupta created a strong central authority, which resided in the capital of his empire, Pataliputra. He ruled with a council of ministers, with Chanakya as the chief minister. This central authority ruled the entire empire, divided into janapadas (territories). Each territory was protected and secured with forts. The administration was layered, as Chandragupta employed tax collectors, spies, jurors, councilors, and even law officers, which would have been similar to modern-day police officers. Chandragupta's law officers were supposed to keep law and order across the empire; this is why the crime rate was meager. The empire also had an administration for agriculture, cities, and the military. Each worked simultaneously to keep the empire running smoothly. Chandragupta frequently organized sacrifices in the religious realm following Vedic tradition and Brahmin rituals. He also planned religious festivals, including processions with horses and elephants throughout the capital. Chandragupta would rarely leave the palace. Chanakya was aware of the dangers of being king, and he knew that potential assassins could try to kill Chandragupta. To keep the king safe, Chanakya created strategies to protect him. Chandragupta was allowed to attend sacrifices and ritual ceremonies publicly. He was also very tolerant of every religion, and many religions thrived during his reigns, like Buddhism, Jainism, Hinduism, and Ajvika, alongside Brahmanism.

Chandragupta could leave the safety of his palace for important government business and military campaigns. To evade potential assassins, he often changed his bedroom. Chanakya, his advisor, took extra precautions to protect Chandragupta from court conspiracies. When the king went hunting, he was accompanied by a special unit of all-female guards, as they were perceived to be less likely to engage in court intrigue. During religious ceremonies, he was surrounded by male guards. The safety of the king was a top priority, but so was the economy of the Maurya Empire.

Chandragupta built numerous water tanks, irrigation systems, temples, and roads to ensure the entire population could get food and other supplies. The king also used these roads to send supplies to the forces far from home. This practice would become one of Chandragupta's many legacies, as other successors to the throne would consider it a standard. The empire depended greatly on trading, and Chandragupta created trading networks, manufacturing centers, and broader roads more suitable for transporting goods in carts. Evidence of multiple miles-long highways leading in and out of the empire to Nepal, Taxila, Dehradun, Odisha, Mirzapur, Kapilavastu, Karnataka, and Andhra. The capitals of Pataliputra and Taxila were directly connected by a thousand-mile-long highway, which was used for commerce, travel, and postal transportation.

The highway was known as Uttarapath. It is somewhat peculiar that there is little evidence of art and elaborate architecture in the Maurya Empire. Archaeologists have not been able to find many remains of art except for scriptures scriptures that Chanakya and Megasthenes mostly wrote. Megasthenes was a Greek historian and an ambassador of Seleucus I Nicator. He lived at Chandragupta's court, serving as an Indian ethnographer. Megasthenes wrote a book about his exploration of India called Indica (also called Indika). The original scripture is lost; however, some fragments were retrieved by archaeologists.

Chandragupta was a remarkable individual who rose from humble beginnings to become a great emperor. His extraordinary life could easily have gone unnoticed in history, but through his partnership with Chanakya, he transformed everything and established the largest native Indian empire. Not only was Chandragupta an exceptional ruler, but he was also deeply loved by his people. He implemented a complex and effective bureaucracy and prioritized the welfare of his citizens.

His legacy is significant; his reign, along with that of his descendants, marked an era of economic prosperity, reforms, and infrastructure expansion. This included the development of irrigation systems, roads, and mines throughout the empire, fostering flourishing trade, commerce, and agriculture. Chandragupta was also known for his religious tolerance, allowing various faiths to thrive during his rule, including Buddhism, Jainism, Hinduism, Ajvika, and Brahmanism.

Chandragupta and Chanakya first established a strong central administration to unify the empire. They created parallel government structures to meet the needs of both rural and urban areas effectively. The military was crucial, leading to the formation of an entire administrative body dedicated to its oversight. They encouraged trade and commerce, monopolizing weapons manufacturing while allowing private mining operators to compete for contracts. Tax breaks stimulated economic activity, as Chanakya believed that excessive taxation could incite rebellion among the citizens.

Shravanabelagola 2007

The road systems they developed aided troop movements and strengthened the administration of a vast empire while facilitating trade, commerce, and internal migration between urban centers. Additionally, they introduced progressive reforms for their time, including state provisions for vulnerable groups such as pregnant women, the elderly, and disabled individuals, as well as for those affected by natural disasters. Laws were also established allowing individuals to divorce and remarry, with a particular emphasis on not prohibiting such practices for widows.

According to Jain sources, Chandra Gupta embraced Jainism towards the end of his life and stepped down from the throne in favor of his son Bindusara. Accompanied by Badrabahu, a Jain Monk, and several other monks, he is said to have gone to Shravanabelagola in Karnataka, where he deliberately starved himself to death in the approved Jain tradition. His death is particularly inspiring. According to some prominent historians, he renounced all his wealth and spent five weeks meditating, reflecting on his guilt for the lives lost during his conquests. By modern standards, this act positioned him as a figure of great moral depth. Together with Chanakya, he implemented many far-reaching policies that contributed to the empire's prosperity and power.

Chandragupta Maurya is one of the greatest Indian rulers, deserving recognition alongside prominent figures such as Ashoka, Rajaraja Chola, and Chhatrapati Shivaji Maharaj.

BINDUSARA (320 BCE—273 BCE)

Bindusara, also known as Amitraghata, was the second Mauryan emperor of India. He was the son of Chandragupta and Durdhara, the daughter of Dhana Nanda, and the father of one of India's most renowned rulers, Ashoka the Great. According to Jain sources,

Bindusara's original name was 'Simhasena.' He was also given several titles, including 'Ajathashatru,' which means 'Man without Enemies.'

Bindusara was a skilled and capable ruler who effectively unified and strengthened the vast empire initiated by his father, Chandragupta Maurya. Historical accounts highlight his ambitious military campaigns across the expansive Deccan Plateau, where his forces advanced towards the southern borders inhabited by the formidable Tamil kingdoms. Although he could not subjugate these regions fully, they recognized his authority and willingly offered tribute, affirming the Mauryan Empire's influential position in the area.

Buddhist and Jain texts mention a legend about how Bindusara got his name. Both accounts state that Chandragupta's minister Chanakya used to mix small doses of poison in the emperor's food to build his immunity against possible poisoning attempts. One day, Chandragupta, not knowing about the poison, shared his food with his pregnant wife. According to the Buddhist legends (*Mahavamsa* and *Mahavamsa Tikka*), the empress was seven days away from delivery. Chanakya arrived just as the empress ate the poisoned morsel. Realizing that she was going to die, he decided to save the unborn child. He cut off the empress's head and cut open her belly with a sword to take out the fetus. Over the next seven days, he placed the fetus in the belly of a goat freshly killed each day. After seven days, Chandragupta's son was "born". He was named Bindusara because his body was spotted with drops ("Bindu") of goat's blood. The Jain text *Parishishta-Parvan* names the empress as Durdhara and states that Chanakya entered the room the very moment she collapsed. To save the child, he cut open the dead empress's womb and took the baby out. By this time, a drop ("*bindu*") of poison had already reached the baby and touched its head. Therefore, Chanakya named him Bindusara, meaning "the strength of the drop".

As we know, Chandragupta reigned for more than 26 years, leaving behind a large and powerful empire for his 22-year-old son Bindusara to inherit. Chanakya remained his chief advisor and asked Bindusara to appoint a man named Subandhu as one of his ministers. Subandhu was very ambitious and wanted to become a minister of higher status. He grew jealous of Chanakya. To take revenge, he told Bindusara that Chanakya had cut open the belly of his mother at the time of his birth. After confirming the story, Bindusara began to hate Chanakya, but in due course, Bindusara learned about the detailed circumstances of his birth and implored Chanakya to resume his ministerial duties. When Chanakya refused, The Emperor ordered Subandhu to soothe him. Still, while pretending to appease Chanakya, he burned him to death, and so was the end of one of the greatest political thinkers in history. Shortly after, due to Chanakya's curse, Subhandhu had to retire and become a monk.

Bindusara, like his father, was an expansive ruler who conquered large areas of the Deccan Plateau, reaching as far south as Mysore. He maintained good relations with the Hellenic states in the West, a legacy established by his father. Bindusara nearly unified the entire Indian Peninsula, with the exception of Kalinga, which was later conquered by his son Ashoka, along with the Tamil Kingdoms. He was commonly known as the king who conquered the two lands between the two seas—the Arabian Sea and the Bay of Bengal.

ASHOKA THE GREAT (268 BCE—232 BCE)

Ashoka was the greatest monarch of India and one of the most significant emperors in the world. He was the third emperor of the Mauryan Empire and the first historically documented emperor of India. Ashoka succeeded his father, Bindusara, and became the Mauryan King in 268 B.C.

ASHOKA PILLAR STUPA 1

DE VĀ NAM PI YA SA A SO KA

Devanampiyasa Asoka

Bindusara's reign was one of peace and relative stability, but when he died, the kingdom was thrust into a brief interregnum over who would be the next king. Historians are still divided on what exactly took place after Bindusara died. The Buddhist sources provide the bulk of the information for this short period. Still, they could be described as "pseudo-historical" at best, as they are more concerned with presenting the Buddhist emperor Ashoka as an enlightened ruler despite his shortcomings. Many modern scholars believe that after Bindusara died or was possibly murdered, a four-year civil war was fought among his brothers for control of the Mauryan Dynasty. The rightful heir to Bindusara was a man named Susuma. However, the capital city of Pataliputra—home to the royal crown, treasury, and army—was occupied by Ashoka, another son of Bindusara. Since Ashoka occupied the metaphorical high ground, he eventually defeated all rival claimants to the throne and made himself the ruler of most of India.

Ashoka was known only as a figure mentioned in the Puranas for a long time. However, in 1837 A.D., James Princep deciphered an inscription written in

Brahmi script that referred to a king named "Devanampiya Piyadasi." Subsequently, many more similar inscriptions were discovered. Initially, these records could not be definitively attributed to Ashoka. However, in 1915, another inscription specifically mentioned Ashoka Piyadasi. This discovery was corroborated by the Ceylonese Chronicle, Mahavamsa, which confirmed that Ashoka, the Mauryan monarch, was referred to as Devanampiya Piyadassi in his inscriptions. According to Buddhist sources, Ashoka usurped the throne after killing rival claimants and began his reign as a tyrant. However, his inscriptions do not support this, which constitutes an important source for studying Mauryan history.

BATTLE OF KALINGA (261 B.C.)

The most important event of Asoka's reign was the battle of Kalinga. This victorious war was responsible for his conversion to Buddhism. The battle of Kalinga was the first and last war waged by Ashoka. It was waged in the eight year, after his coronation. The 13th Major Rock Edict gives details about this battle. "When he had been consecrated eight years, the Beloved of Gods, the King Piyadassi, conquered Kalinga." The horror of the war is described in Asoka's own words: "A hundred and fifty thousand people were deported, a hundred thousand were killed, and many more died." Some scholars would have us believe that Ashoka, moved by untold miseries caused by the war, dramatically embraced Buddhism. However, according to his inscriptions, only after two and a half years did he become an enthusiastic supporter of Buddhism.

RESULTS OF WAR:: The Kalinga War had a profound impact on Ashoka, leading him to renounce war as a strategy for conquest. During his reign, the Buddhist Church gained recognition, marked by the convening of the Third Buddhist Council in Pataliputra around 250 B.C., under the leadership of a Buddhist monk and scholar named Moggali Putta Thissa. Following his conquest of Kalinga, Ashoka experienced deep remorse; he recognized the immense suffering caused by the slaughter, death, and displacement of the people when an independent nation was conquered.

In a transformative shift, Ashoka reached out to the tribal communities and the neighboring frontier kingdoms with a heartfelt ideological appeal. He spoke to the people of the independent states in Kalinga, urging them to see him not merely as a ruler but as a father figure who genuinely cared for their well-being and sought their trust. Abandoning the traditional view of foreign territories as mere conquests ripe for a military takeover, Ashoka instead adopted a progressive approach aimed at winning over the hearts and minds of these distant lands through ideology and compassion.

He embarked on a series of significant initiatives focused on the welfare of both people and animals, advocating for a more harmonious and ethical society. This approach was groundbreaking for his time, as he prioritized peaceful coexistence and mutual respect over the aggression and violence that often characterized the relationships between empires and their neighbors. Through these efforts, Ashoka sought to sow the seeds of goodwill and understanding beyond his borders, marking a remarkable departure from conventional imperial ambitions. However, viewing the Kalinga War as making Ashoka an extreme pacifist would be incorrect. His pursuit of peace was not unconditional; instead, he adopted a pragmatic approach focused on consolidating his empire. After conquering Kalinga, he retained and incorporated the region into his empire.

HIS SUCCESSORS: The Mauryan Empire began to decline slowly after Ashoka's reign. Seven successors followed him and ruled for fifty years. The last Mauryan king, Brihadratha, was killed by Pushyamitra Sunga in 180 B.C., which marked the beginning of the Shunga dynasty.

SOURCES OF MAURYAN HISTORY

THE ARTHASHASTRA

The Arthashastra, written by Kautilya, is essential for studying Mauryan history. It provides a comprehensive overview of the period's Mauryan polity, administrative system, and social and economic conditions. The text, written in Sanskrit, was discovered by Dr. Shama Shastri in 1905 A.D. at the Oriental Library in Mysore.

The Arthashastra contains 150 chapters and 6,000 shlokas. The second chapter discusses civil administration, while the third and fourth chapters shed light on civil and criminal procedures. The fourteenth chapter describes the Mauryan polity and the seventh and fifteenth chapters outline the relationship between the Mauryan state and other states. In addition to these aspects, the Arthashastra details the Mauryan period's economy, professions, architecture, and other elements.

Kautilya, in the Arthashastra, advocates for an absolute monarchy. He introduces the "saptanga" theory of kingship, which includes seven key components: Swami (the king), Amatya (the minister), Kosha (the treasury), Bala (the military), Janapada (the people), Durga (the fortifications), and Mitra (the allies). Kautilya advises that a king should embody a fox's cunning, a crow's intelligence, and a lion's courage. He highlights the importance of having a council of ministers to assist the king in governance and recommends the establishment of a secretariat with eighteen departments for effective administration.

THE BOOK "INDICA" OF MEGASTHENES

Megasthenes, a Greek general and ambassador of Seleukos Niketor, lived for many years at the Mauryan court in Pataliputra and traveled extensively throughout India. He recorded his observations in his book, "Indica." Although the full text of "Indica" is not available to us, many Greek writers have referenced various facts contained within it. However, Megasthenes' lack of familiarity with the Indian context means that some of his observations were not entirely accurate. He did not understand the Indian languages, traditions, or geography, yet his accounts still provide valuable information.

His description of the city administration of Pataliputra is noteworthy. According to Megasthenes, Pataliputra was a major metropolis, located at the confluence of the Ganges and Soan rivers, measuring 9.5 miles in length and 1.5 miles in width. The city was surrounded by a wooden wall and featured a trench that was sixty feet deep and 600 feet wide.

The administration of Pataliputra was managed by a committee of thirty members, which was divided into six subcommittees with five members each. Additionally, Megasthenes mentions a war council consisting of thirty members. He categorized Indian society into seven divisions: philosophers, peasants, pastoralists, artisans, soldiers, officials, and ministers. However, he likely misunderstood the Indian social structure, as he seemed to equate various professions with castes.

Despite these shortcomings, Megasthenes' accounts are still regarded as a valuable source for studying Mauryan history.

MUDRA RAKSHASA OF VISAKADUTTA

The political drama written by Vishaka Dutta in the 5th century A.D. during the Gupta period is an important work related to the history of the Mauryan period. It details how Chandragupta Maurya received the assistance of Kautilya to overthrow the Nanda dynasty. Additionally, the play provides insights into the social, economic, and religious life of the Mauryan period. Although this work was not composed during the Mauryan era, the author made a significant effort to base the drama on the information available in the 5th century A.D., much of which is now lost.

Jain traditions tell us that Chandragupta Maurya embraced Jainism towards the end of his reign and abdicated his throne. Similarly, Buddhist traditions highlight the steps he took to promote this faith.

ASHOKAS ROCK EDICTS

Ashoka was the first Indian ruler to introduce inscriptions to develop moral and ethical values among the people. So, he was called the father of inscriptions in India. These inscriptions were inscribed on rocks and pillars by Ashoka throughout his empire. The languages used in these inscriptions were Prakrit mixed with Pali and Greek. The major scripts were Brahmi, Kharosti, and Greek. The inscriptions in India and Nepal were written in Brahmi script and Kharosti scripts in Afghanistan and Arabicakistan. Aramic script originated in ancient Syria and was used in the inscriptions of Kandahar.

CATEGORIES OF EDICTS: (INSCRIPTIONS) 14 major rock edicts 7 Pillar edicts 2 Kalinga edicts 2 Minor Pillar inscriptions 2 Minor inscriptions 2 Commemorative minor pillar edicts and cave edicts.

FOURTEEN MAJOR ROCK EDICTS

These edicts describe the nature of Asoka's administration and the moral status of his empire. The important places of these edicts were Girnar, Dhauli, Jaugada, Sophara, Erragudi, Shabazgaril and Mansera.

SEVEN PILLAR EDICTS

These edicts were found at Topra in Haryana, Meerut,, and Champaran. The Pillar edicts repeated the contents of the major rock edicts. Two Kalinga edicts were found at Dhauli and Jaugada in Orissa. These edicts explain Ashoka's new administrative system after the battle of Kalinga.

TWO MINOR ROCK EDICTS

The first edict explains Ashoka's personal life, and the second gives information about Asoka's Dharma Policy. They are the Babru edict and the Maski inscription. The Babru edict justifies Asoka's conversion to Buddhism, and the Maski edict refers to Ashoka as Devanampiya Priyadarshini Ashoka.

FOUR MINOR PILLAR EDICTS

These inscriptions were found at Sarnath, Allahabad in Uttar Pradesh, Sanchi in Madhya Pradesh, and Amaravati in Andhra Pradesh. Two Commemorative minor pillar edicts were found at Rummindei and Nigalisagar in Nepal. They justify Ashoka's policies regarding the spread of Buddhism and mention his Dharma yatras.

CAVE INSCRIPTIONS

Cave inscriptions are found in the Barabar caves of Jehanabad district in Bihar. There are two caves known as Barabar and Nagarjuni. The Nagarjuni group has three caves, one of which has the inscriptions of Asoka's grandson, Dasharatha Devanampiya. The Barbara group has four caves, one of which has the inscriptions of Ashoka.

His minor rock edicts were also located in Rupanath (Madhya Pradesh), Sasaram (Bihar), Bairat (Jaipura), Rajula Mundagiri (Andhra Pradesh), Gujarat, Brahmagiri, Jatinga, Rameshwaram, Gavimatta, and Pakigunda (Karnataka). Among these, the Gujarara inscriptions contain Ashoka's name and title as Devanpiya Ashoka Rajasa.

THE ADMINISTRATION OF THE MAURYA EMPIRE

Chandragupta Maurya laid the foundation for an efficient administration system during the Mauryan period, which continued to function smoothly with minimal changes. The administrative system under Ashoka was mainly similar to that established by his grandfather, Chandragupta Maurya. However, Ashoka placed particular emphasis on the parental principles of governance. Key texts such as Kautilya's "Arthashastra," Megasthenes' "Indica," and the Ashokan edicts are significant sources for understanding the Mauryan administration.

CENTRAL GOVERNMENT

The King: The king was the highest authority in the state, wielding unlimited power. He served as the supreme judge, with final authority over all judicial matters. The king led the military and deliberated on offense and defense strategies with his commander-in-chief. His pronouncements were considered law, and he was seen as the fountainhead of justice. The king received credit for any happiness provided to the people but acknowledged that he was not above the law; instead, dharma was sovereign. His duty was to punish those who disobeyed the laws. He was not an autocrat, and he adhered to established laws. He acted as a father figure to his subjects, prioritizing their welfare and maintaining law and order. While making important decisions, he consulted others.

According to Megasthenes, his palace was beautifully designed and adorned with parks, artificial lakes, and various comforts. Kautilya notes that Chandragupta dedicated special attention to numerous public benefit projects. Although Ashoka did not pursue a policy of military conquests, he ultimately ruled over a vast empire.

Council of Ministers (Mantri Parishad): The king was assisted in his duties by the Mantri Parishad or council of ministers. Kautilya emphasized the importance of appointing ministers, stating in the Arthashastra that "a single wheel cannot move alone," thus promoting the need for ministers. These ministers were wise, loyal, and of high character, providing beneficial counsel to the king and his subjects. Kautilya advised kings to always consult their ministers while retaining their autonomy and not becoming mere puppets. The council of ministers functioned primarily as an advisory body, with meetings held in complete secrecy, based on Kautilya's belief that "even walls have ears." Each minister was responsible for a specific department and was accountable for its effective management.

The most influential ministers in the council included the Prime Minister (Amatya), the Commander-in-Chief (Senapati), the Chief Priest (Purohita), and the

Crown Prince (Yuvaraj). The king and his ministers were supported by many officials who ensured the efficient functioning of the government. The Central Government had eighteen departments, each headed by different officers. The officers were known by different names. They were: **1.** Sannidata (Treasurer) **2.** Samharta (Tax collector) **3.** Prathihara **4.** Sithadhyaksha (Land revenue collector) **5.** Sitadhyyaksha (Chief of excise department) **6.** Durgapala (Manager of Royal Palace) **7.** Antapala (Supervisor of border ports) **8.** Prashasta (State record keeper) **9.** Ashapataladhyaksha (Chief accounts officer)

Some separate officers looked after trade, forest, mint, octroi, etc. Each officer was required to ensure that the state did not lose anything and that people's interests were fully protected.

MILITARY ADMINISTRATION:

From all available records, it appears the king maintained a powerful army, often led by the king himself. The army was controlled by a Commander-in-Chief, or Senapati, who was as powerful as the Prime Minister, or Amatya. The Mauryan army consisted of 600,000 infantry, 30,000 cavalry, 8,000 chariots, and 9,000 elephants. Each chariot carried two soldiers. The troops were well-equipped, but the king relied more on elephants and cavalry than infantry. The soldiers were armed with swords, shields, bows, lances, and other weapons.

According to Megasthenes, the army's affairs were managed by a council of thirty members, divided into six boards, each consisting of five members. There was one board each for the navy, transport, infantry, elephants, and chariots. The Navy Board managed ships, dealt with pirates, and collected taxes from merchants, with its chief designated as Navadhyaksha. The Transport Board was responsible for military logistics, including the bullock carts maintained by the state.

The Board for Infantry managed the infantry soldiers, while the Cavalry Board, headed by Asvadhyaksha, was in charge of the horsemen. The Board for Elephants, led by Rathadhyaksha, oversaw the elephant force, and a separate board handled war chariots under Rathadhyaksha's leadership. This was the first time an Indian ruler maintained such a large standing army. The army proved quite efficient, successfully defeating Seleucus and achieving notable victories for Ashoka in the Kalinga War.

ESPIONAGE SYSTEM:

The efficient operation of the Mauryan administrative machinery relied heavily on spies, who were both capable and loyal. These spies kept the king informed about events within his empire and neighboring states and public opinion on various important matters. Many of these spies were women, as Kautilya believed they could be more effective than men in such roles. According to Arian, the spies of Chandragupta Maurya were highly dependable.

JUDICIAL ADMINISTRATION:

The Mauryan kings took a keen interest in the administration of justice. Megasthenes noted that Chandragupta Maurya sometimes spent the whole day hearing cases and giving judgments. Regular courts were established across the country. In villages, disputes were resolved by Village Panchayats, while cities had city courts. Appeals from these courts could be made to provincial courts and from there to the central court located in Patliputra. Cases were not decided summarily; a system for summoning witnesses was also in place. The laws were quite severe, with punishments ranging from simple fines to shaving of hair, cutting off limbs, public humiliation, whipping, and even capital punishment. No leniency was shown to offenders.

There were three types of local courts: those formed by citizens to settle disputes, those established by business guilds, and those created by village assemblies. These local courts helped facilitate the resolution of conflicts. The Arthashastra mentions two specific courts: Dharmasthiya, which handled civil laws like inheritance, marriage disputes, etc., and Kantaksodhana, which dealt with criminal cases. Provincial courts were also located in important district towns.

In the administration of justice, it was believed that the guilty should be punished severely, often through torture or whipping. As a result, crime rates were quite low.

Regarding revenue administration, the Mauryan government maintained that the treasury should be completely full and overflowing, as this was essential for the welfare of the people. Land revenue was the primary source of the government's income, varying based on the fertility and location of the land. It typically amounted to a percentage of the total agricultural produce.

Other sources of revenue included land tax, dues from mines, forests, and cattle, tolls, ferry duties, professional fees, fines, and gifts. The officer responsible for finances and revenue collection was known as the Samharta.

The main sources of expenditure were social welfare activities, state administration, including maintenance of law and order, payment of armed forces, etc.

PROVINCIAL ADMINISTRATION:

The Mauryan Empire was very vast in its extent and was therefore divided into four main provinces:

1. The Northern Province, with its capital at Taxila.

2. The Western Province, known as Avanti Rashtra, with its capital at Ujjain.

3. The Eastern Province of Kalinga, with its capital at Tosali.

4. The Southern Province, with its capital at Suvarnagiri., also known as Kanakagiri, in present-day Karnataka.

There was also a fifth province known as Magadha, or Prashi, which was directly governed by the king. Governors managed the other provinces, typically members of the royal family, called Kumaramatyas. The structure of the provincial government closely mirrored that of the central government. Numerous officials were appointed to assist in the administration of these provinces.

In addition to the provinces, there were feudatory states known as samanthas. These states acknowledged the king's supremacy but were permitted to govern as they wished. However, they were required to pay annual tributes and recognize the king's authority.

LOCAL ADMINISTRATION

The provinces were further divided into districts. Each district was under Sthanika, who was helped by Gopa and, in turn, assisted by the village elders. The minor unit administration was a village. It was under the charge of Gramika. At times, he was either elected or nominated by the government. There was a village assembly that helped Gramika discharge their duties. The office of the Gramika was honorary. Gopa, it appears, was above the Gramika, and above Gopa was Sthanika, who supervised the work of the district. From all accounts, it seems that village administration was very efficient. The king did not interfere in village affairs but ensured that administration worked systematically and each senior person was a check on the other.

THE DHAMMA OR DHARMA OF ASHOKA :

After the Kalinga War, Ashoka decided to embrace Buddhism and renounce violence and warfare. He began visiting significant Buddhist pilgrimage sites, including Bodh Gaya, Lumbini Gardens (the birthplace of Buddha), Kapilavastu, and Sarnath. Instead of pursuing military conquests (digvijaya), he chose to focus on the victory of righteousness (dharmavijaya). Ashoka took various steps to promote Buddhism and propagate the principles of dharma, or Dhamma.

While Buddhism was Ashoka's personal faith, he did not impose it on his subjects. Instead, he preached an essence that encompassed not just Buddhism but also fundamental principles from various religions. Thus, Ashoka's concept of Dhamma differed from traditional Buddhism.

The essence of Dhamma comprised a collection of valuable principles from all religions, focusing on ethics that were not exclusive to Buddhism. According to R.D. Tripathi, "Nowhere in his edicts does Ashoka mention the Four Noble Truths, the Eightfold Path, or the goal of Nirvana." Ashoka outlined these moral rules to enhance the purity and happiness of his subjects' lives.

One of the main principles of Ashoka's Dhamma was respect for elders, which is also referenced in the Upanishads through the phrases: "Matru Devo Bhava, Pitru Devo Bhava, Acharya Devo Bhava, and Atithi Devo Bhava." Furthermore, Ashoka's concepts of monarchy, religious tolerance, and ahimsa (non-violence) have parallels in works such as the Arthashastra, Sigalovada Sutta, and Sutta Nipata.

The objectives of the Dhamma Policy included fostering harmony among people of different religions and encouraging social good conduct. One reason for adopting this broader concept of dharma is believed to be maintaining the unity and integrity of the empire.

CAUSES FOR THE DOWNFALL OF THE MAURYAN EMPIRE

The Mauryan Empire began to decline after the death of Ashoka in 232 BC. Following his death, the empire was divided into Western and Eastern halves, leading to a civil war over succession. Ashoka's firstborn son, Mahendra, went on to spread Buddhism across the world. His second son, Kunala Maurya, was blind and, therefore, could not ascend to the throne, and his third son, Kaurwaki, died before Ashoka died. The Mauryan territories in the Deccan declared independence under the Satavahanas, and Kalinga reemerged as a separate entity. In 180 BC, just 50 years after Ashoka's death, Brihadrath, the ninth Mauryan emperor, inspected his army while accompanied by his commander-in-chief, Pushyamitra Shunga. The Mauryan Empire was not as strong after the time of Ashoka. It experienced significant political instability, with six Mauryan kings being enthroned and dethroned in just 50 years. This volatility led to Pushyamitra Shunga seizing power; he assassinated Brihadrath Maurya, and the Shungas became the new emperors of Magadha.

According to H.P. Sastri, the primary reason for the decline of the Mauryan Empire can be traced back to Emperor Ashoka's anti-Brahmanical policies. Ashoka's profound interest in Buddhism led him to pursue reforms that included the abolition of animal sacrifices, a practice deeply rooted in Brahmanical tradition. This shift marginalized the Brahmanas, who had long held a position of superiority in society, leading to increasing resentment towards Ashoka. Feeling threatened and disadvantaged, the Brahmanas began to conspire against him, ultimately plotting the empire's downfall. Their opposition proved disastrous, culminating in the assassination of the last Mauryan ruler, Brihadratha, by a Brahmin general named Pushya Mitra Sunga.

In contrast, D.D. Kosambi presents a different perspective, arguing that the fundamental cause behind the Mauryan Empire's collapse was its financial frailty. Managing a vast empire necessitated a large standing army and a sprawling bureaucracy, both of which imposed significant costs on the state. To sustain itself, the Mauryan administration levied heavy taxes on its subjects, placing an enormous financial burden on the populace. Following Ashoka's death, the once-sturdy bureaucratic system began to deteriorate, succumbing to corruption and inefficiency. This decline in administrative integrity further exacerbated the financial pressures, significantly contributing to the eventual disintegration of the empire.

The news of the fall of the Mauryan Empire sent shockwaves throughout South Asia. This central power vacuum allowed new dynasties to emerge across India. In the north, the Indo-Greeks invaded; in the east, the Chedis took control, and in the south, the Satavahanas grew stronger. For the next few centuries, these powers—both native and foreign—were engaged in a continuous struggle.

According to the Ashokavadana, Pushyamitra Shunga aspired to be more revered than Ashoka and sought to erase his achievements. As a result, he ordered the destruction of the stupas that Ashoka had constructed and began persecuting the Buddhist monks he had once supported. His destructive actions extended from Sakala (modern-day Sialkot) to Sanchi, possibly even Kaushambi (near present-day Prayagraj).

CHAPTER 10
THE CLASSICAL PERIOD PART 1

When Emperor Ashoka passed away in 232 BCE, he left behind a vast and predominantly Buddhist empire, home to approximately 30 million people. Ashoka, known for his commitment to moral governance and the promotion of Buddhist values, had significantly influenced the culture and administration of his realm. His death, however, marked the onset of a gradual decline in both the prominence of Buddhism and the stability of the Mauryan Empire.

In the immediate aftermath of Ashoka's death, the first signs of fragmentation appeared when Taxila, a major city and cultural center, seceded from the empire. The city's leaders cited an increasing burden of oppressive taxation as their primary grievance, setting a precedent for other regions. Taxila's breakaway was the first of many discontented regions to distance themselves from the empire, which Chandragupta Maurya and his lineage had intricately weaved together.

Within half a century of Ashoka's demise, around 180 BCE, the Mauryan Empire faced further turmoil with the assassination of its last emperor, Brihadatta. This critical event was orchestrated by Pushyamitra Shunga, a general influenced by power struggles and the declining authority of the Mauryan rulers. With Brihadatta's death, the Shunga Empire emerged, marking the transition toward a new political order characterized by its expansion across the northern regions of the Indian subcontinent. This change coincided with the resurgence of Greek conquests, which introduced a new layer of complexity and competition to the evolving dynamics of power in the region.

The period that began in about 200 BC did not witness a large empire like the Mauryas, but it is notable for intimate and widespread contacts between Central Asia and India. In the eastern and central parts of India and the Deccan, the Mauryas were succeeded by several native rulers, such as the Shungas, the Kanvas, and the Satavahanas. In north-western India, they were succeeded by several ruling dynasties from Central Asia. Of them, the Kushans became the most famous.

THE SHUNGAS

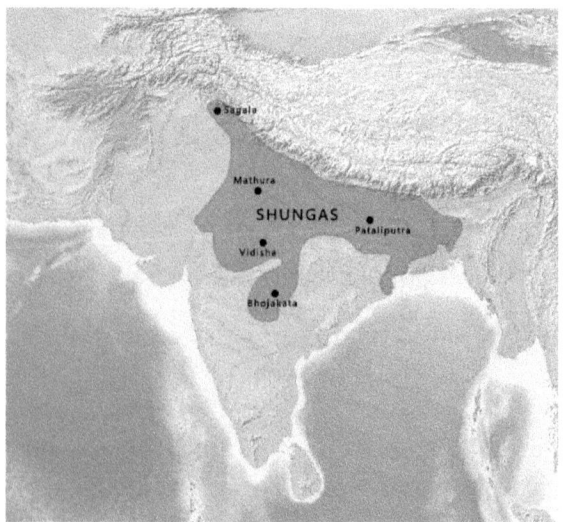

Shunga Empire Extent

Shunga Mother with Child

According to the Harshacharita, Pushyamitra, the commander-in-chief of the Maurya army, killed the Maurya king Brihadratha while the latter was inspecting his troops. This coup marked the end of Maurya's rule in India. The Puranas describe Pushyamitra as belonging to the Shunga family. There are several references to Shunga teachers in Vedic texts, including a mention of a teacher named Shaungiputra in the Brihadaranyaka Upanishad. Panini links the Shungas to the Brahmana

Bharadvaja gotra. Additionally, Kalidasa's Malavikagnimitra describes Agnimitra, the son of Pushyamitra, as belonging to the Baimbika kula (family/lineage) and Kashyapa gotra. While these sources vary in detail, they all indicate that the Shungas were Brahmanas.

Pushyamitra's empire represented a significant portion of the former Maurya Empire, primarily encompassing important regions like Pataliputra, which continued as the capital, as well as Ayodhya and Vidisha. Historical accounts, particularly from the Divyavadana and Taranatha, suggest that his empire extended further into Punjab, reaching regions such as Jalandhara and Shakala. Understanding the governance of his empire, it is noted that Pushyamitra appointed viceroys to oversee various territories. For example, in the ancient drama Malavikagnimitra, a character named Agnimitra is depicted as the viceroy of Vidisha, indicating organized administration under Pushyamitra's reign.

The narrative of the Shungas is marked by several conflicts, particularly against external forces like the Bactrian Greeks. A notable reference comes from the works of the 2nd-century BCE grammarian Patanjali, who discusses the arrival of the Yavanas—a term that, during this period, broadly referred to western foreigners, particularly the Greeks. Patanjali mentions their presence in Saketa (believed to be in or around present-day Ayodhya, Uttar Pradesh) and Madhyamika (near Chittor in Rajasthan). In this instance, the term Yavana specifically identifies the Bactrian Greeks who had begun to establish their influence in the Indian subcontinent.

Further illustrating this conflict, Malavikagnimitra recounts a dramatic military encounter that took place on the banks of the Sindhu River, involving Prince Vasumitra, the son of Agnimitra. Scholars continue to debate whether the Sindhu is referred to as the Indus River itself or another river located in central India. This military confrontation occurred amidst the backdrop of Pushyamitra's Ashvamedha sacrifice, a significant ritual involving the release of a consecrated horse, which was then challenged by the Yavana forces. The drama penned by Kalidasa portrays a resounding victory for Pushyamitra, showcasing the young prince's bravery and military skill as he successfully safeguards the horse and returns it home.

Questions remain regarding the identity of the Bactrian Greek leader involved in these skirmishes. Historical figures such as Menander, Demetrius, and Eukratides have been proposed as candidates, although Demetrius is frequently considered the most likely leader during this tumultuous period.

In addition to military exploits, the Ayodhya stone inscription attributed to King Dhana emphasizes Pushyamitra's dedicated performance of two ashvamedha sacrifices, underscoring his status and legitimacy as a ruler. However, the Divyavadana paints a more complex picture of Pushyamitra, detailing accounts of his alleged cruelty and his vehement opposition to Buddhism, suggesting a ruler whose reign was marked by both religious and political ambition.

According to historical sources, ten Shunga kings ruled over a span of approximately 112 years. The Puranic texts indicate that the last monarch of this lineage was either known as Devabhuti or Devabhumi. A significant event in Shunga history is chronicled in the Harshacharita, which describes how Devabhuti became the target of a conspiracy orchestrated by his Brahmana minister, Vasudeva. This plot ultimately led to the downfall of the Shunga dynasty and the rise of the Kanva dynasty as Vasudeva seized power.

It is noteworthy that even after the collapse of the Shunga rule, remnants of their influence likely persisted in central India for some time, paving the way for the emergence of the Satavahanas. Eventually, the Kanvas were succeeded by the Mitras in Magadha, and the Mitras themselves would later be dislodged by the Shakas, further illustrating the dynamic and ever-changing landscape of ancient Indian political history.

THE INDO-GREEKS

A series of invasions began around 200 BC, with the first to cross the Hindu Kush being the Greeks, who ruled Bactria (or Bahlika), located south of the Oxus River in present-day northern Afghanistan. These invasions occurred one after another, though some invaders ruled simultaneously. A significant factor contributing to these invasions was the weakness of the Seleucid Empire, which had been established in Bactria and the adjacent area of Iran known as Parthia. As the Scythian tribes exerted increasing pressure, later Greek rulers struggled to maintain control over the region.

With the construction of the Great Wall of China, the Scythians were pushed back from the Chinese border and redirected their focus toward the neighboring

Greeks and Parthians. As a result, pressured by the Scythians, the Bactrian Greeks were compelled to invade India. The successors of Ashoka were too weak to prevent the foreign invasions that began during this period.

The first invaders of India were the Greeks, referred to as the Indo-Greeks or Indo-Bactrians. By the beginning of the second century BC, the Indo-Greeks occupied a significant portion of northwestern India, a much larger area than that conquered by Alexander. Reports suggest that they advanced in Ayodhya and Pataliputra. However, the Greeks were unable to establish a unified rule in India; instead, two Greek dynasties ruled northwestern India simultaneously.

The most notable Indo-Greek ruler was Menander (165–45 BC), also known as Milinda. He established his capital at Sakala (modern-day Sialkot) in Punjab and invaded the Ganga-Yamuna doab, encompassing many cities, including Sakala and Mathura. Menander is known for the extensive variety of coins circulated in his realm. He embraced Buddhism, influenced by Nagasena (also known as Nagarjuna), who engaged in a famous dialogue with him. Their exchanges were recorded in a book known as the "Milinda Panho" or "The Questions of Milinda."

The Indo-Greek rule is significant in Indian history due to the many coins the Greeks issued. They were the first rulers in India to mint coins that could be definitively linked to individual kings, a feat not possible with the earlier punch-marked coins, which cannot be attributed with certainty to any particular dynasty. The

Indo-Greeks were also the first to issue gold coins in India, and their production increased under the Kushans.

Greek rule introduced elements of Hellenistic art to the northwestern frontier of India. However, this cultural interchange was not purely Greek; it resulted from Greek contact with the non-Greek peoples they conquered after Alexander's death. The best example of this fusion of cultures is found in Gandhara art.

THE SATVAHANAS

COIN OF SATKARNI

Historians have emphasized the importance of numismatic evidence, which indicates the existence of numerous small political principalities ('localities') that sprang up in various parts of the Deccan after the decline of the Maurya empire and before the advent of the Satavahanas. Coins of local rulers, often bearing the title maharathi, have been found in stratigraphic contexts at sites such as Verrapuram at pre-Satavahana and Satavahana levels. At Brahmapuri, coins of Kura rulers have been found at pre-Satavahana levels. Unstratified coin finds at Kotalingala give the names of several local rulers such as Gobhadra, Samigopa, Chimuka, Kamvaya, and Narana. A raja named Khubiraka is mentioned in a late 2nd-century BCE inscription found on a relic casket at Bhattiprolu. All this suggests a significant increase in the power and status of local elites during the 2nd–1st centuries BCE.

The Rathikas and Bhojas referenced in Ashoka's inscriptions later evolved into the maharathis and mahabhojas during the pre-Satavahana period. The Satavahanas are believed to correspond with the Andhras described in the Puranas. According to the Matsya and Brahmanda Puranas, 30 kings ruled for a combined total of 460 years, whereas the Vayu Purana records 17 kings ruling for 300 years. It is important to note that some rulers identified through coins and inscriptions do not appear in the Puranic accounts, which complicates the chronology of the dynasty.

Historians continue to engage in spirited debates regarding the precise inception of the Satavahana rule. Some scholars propose that this influential dynasty began its reign around c. 271 BCE, while others suggest a slightly later timeframe, around c. 30 BCE. However, a consensus has emerged that places the commencement of the Satavahana dynasty between the mid-1st century BCE and the early 3rd century CE.

Further complicating this historical narrative is the ongoing discourse about the geographical origins of the Satavahanas. Some researchers contend that they initially carved out their power in the eastern regions of the Deccan Plateau, while others argue for a western genesis. The mention of the term "Andhras" in ancient Puranic texts implies that the Satavahanas might have originated in the Andhra region, or possibly belonged to a tribe associated with it. Additionally, the phrase "Andhra-bhritya," as found in these texts, raises intriguing questions; some historians interpret it as indicating that the ancestors of the Satavahanas were once subordinates of the Maurya Empire, given that "bhritya" translates to "servant" or "subordinate." However, one could also argue that "Andhra-bhritya" means "servants of the Andhras," a term that may refer not only to the Satavahanas but also to their successors.

Archaeological evidence significantly contributes to the ongoing discourse regarding the Satavahana dynasty. The discovery of early Satavahana coins at various sites, including Kotalingala and Sangareddy in the Karimnagar district of Andhra Pradesh, supports the hypothesis that the Satavahanas established their authority in the eastern Deccan region. Conversely, inscriptions located in the Naneghat and Nashik caves suggest that the western Deccan might have served as a formidable base for their early dominance. Therefore, some historians propose that the Satavahanas initially consolidated their influence from the vicinity of Pratishthana, now known as modern Paithan in the western Deccan, before strategically expanding their territory eastward into Andhra and the coastal regions.

The Satavahana Empire ultimately encompassed present-day Andhra Pradesh and Maharashtra, and at times, it extended to include parts of northern Karnataka, eastern and southern Madhya Pradesh, and Saurashtra. The Roman author Pliny references the Andhra region as comprising numerous villages and thirty walled towns, noting that its rulers maintained a substantial military force, including 100,000 infantry, 2,000 cavalry, and 1,000 elephants. Due to the debate surrounding the commencement of Satavahana rule, it is challenging to provide definitive dates for the various rulers of this dynasty; nonetheless, the succession of rulers is relatively well-established. The dynasty's founder, Simuka, was succeeded by his brother Kanha, who notably expanded the empire westward to at least Nashik. The subsequent ruler, Satakarni I, is recognized for his notably lengthy reign, lasting approximately 56 years.

ARCHITECTURE IN THE SATVAHANA PHASE

During the Satavahana phase, numerous chaityas (sacred shrines) and monasteries were skillfully carved out of solid rock in northwestern Deccan, specifically in Maharashtra. This remarkable process began approximately a century earlier, around 200 BC. The two primary forms of religious architecture from this period were the Buddhist temple, known as a chaitya, and the monastery referred to as a vihara. A chaitya was typically a spacious hall supported by several columns, while a vihara featured a central hall accessed through a doorway from a verandah at the front. The most notable chaitya is the one at Karle in the western Deccan, known for its impressive rock architecture, measuring about 40 meters long, 15 meters wide, and 15 meters high.

The viharas, or monasteries, were excavated near the chaityas to serve as residences for monks during the rainy season. In Nasik, there are three viharas that bear inscriptions of Nahapana and Gautamiputra, indicating they date back to the first and second centuries AD.

In addition to viharas, rock-cut architecture is found in Andhra Pradesh, particularly in the Krishna-Godavari region, which is renowned for its independent Buddhist structures, primarily in the form of stupas. The most famous stupas are located at Amaravati and Nagarjunakonda.

The stupa is a large, rounded structure built to house relics of the Buddha. Construction of the Amaravati stupa began around 200 BC, although it underwent complete reconstruction in the latter half of the second century AD. The dome of this stupa measures 53 meters across the base and is believed to be 33 meters tall. The Amaravati stupa is adorned with numerous sculptures depicting various scenes from the Buddha's life.

Nagarjunakonda experienced significant prosperity during the second and third centuries under the patronage of the Ikshvakus, who succeeded the Satavahanas. This site features numerous Buddhist monuments as well as some of the earliest Brahmanical brick temples, with nearly two dozen monasteries still recognizable today. Along with its stupas and mahachaityas, Nagarjunakonda stands out as one of the richest areas in terms of architectural structures during the early centuries of the Christian era.

THE SHAKAS

The Shakas, also known as the Scythians, succeeded the Greeks in power. They effectively dismantled Greek authority in both Bactria and India, controlling a much larger portion of India than the Greeks had. There were five branches of the Shakas, each with their own seat of power spread across various regions of India and Afghanistan.

One branch settled in Afghanistan, the second in Punjab with Taxila as their capital, the third in Mathura, where they ruled for approximately two centuries, the fourth established their hold over western India and continued to rule until the fourth century, and the fifth branch established their power in the upper Deccan. The Shakas did not encounter significant resistance from the local rulers and people of India.

Around 57–58 BC, a king of Ujjain emerged who effectively resisted the Shakas and successfully drove them out during his reign. He adopted the name Vikramaditya, and from his victory in 57 BC, an era known as Vikrama Samvat is calculated. This title of Vikramaditya became highly coveted, similar to how Roman emperors adopted the title Caesar to signify their power. This led to the emergence of as many as fourteen individuals in Indian history who took the name Vikramaditya, with Chandragupta II of the Gupta dynasty being the most renowned among them.

The title remained popular among Indian kings until the twelfth century, especially in western India and the western Deccan. Although the Shakas ruled various regions, only those in western India maintained their power for a significant duration of about four centuries. They benefited from sea-borne trade in Gujarat and minted numerous silver coins.

The most notable Shaka ruler in India was Rudradaman I (AD 130–150). He ruled over Sindh and a considerable part of Gujarat, Konkan, the Narmada valley, Malwa, and Kathiawar. He is particularly remembered for his efforts to repair and enhance the Sudarshana Lake in the semi-arid region of Kathiawar, which had long been utilized for irrigation and dated back to the Mauryan era. Rudradaman was also a great admirer of Sanskrit and, despite having Central Asian ancestry, he issued the first long inscription in pure Sanskrit. Previously, all longer inscriptions in India were composed in Prakrit, which had been established as the state language by Ashoka.

THE PARTHIANS

The Shaka domination in northwestern India was succeeded by that of the Parthians. In several ancient Indian Sanskrit texts, these two groups are mentioned together as the Shaka–Pahlavas, as they ruled over parts of India simultaneously for a period of time. The Parthians, also known as the Pahlavas, originally lived in Iran before migrating to India. Unlike the Greeks and the Shakas, the Parthians controlled only a small portion of northwestern India during the first century AD. The most notable Parthian king was Gondophernes, who is known for the arrival of St. Thomas in India to propagate Christianity during his reign. Over time, like the Shakas before them, the Parthians became an integral part of Indian polity and society.

THE KUSHANS

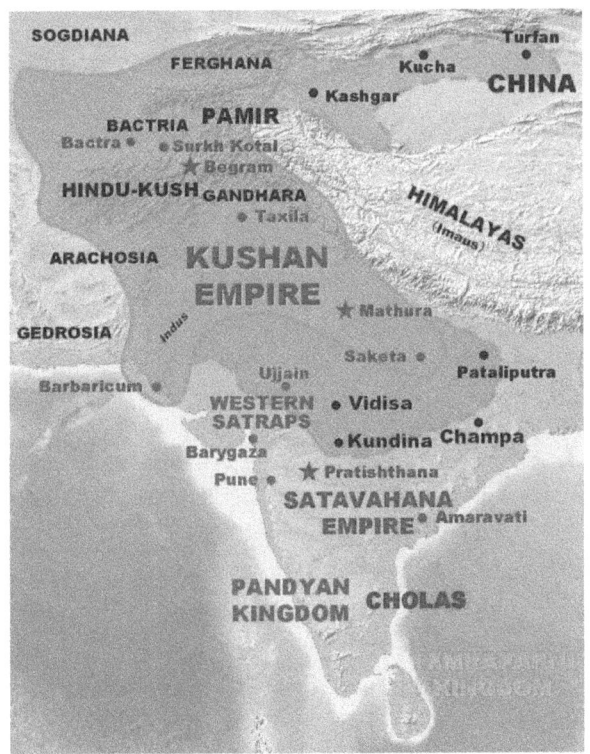

Kushan Map

The Kushans succeeded the Parthians, also known as the Yuechis or Tocharians. The Tocharians are often considered synonymous with the Scythians. The Kushans were one of the five clans that comprised the Yuechi tribe. A nomadic people from the steppes of north-central Asia, the Kushans lived near China and initially occupied Bactria in present-day northern Afghanistan, displacing the Shakas. Gradually, they moved into the Kabul Valley and took control of

Gandhara by crossing the Hindu Kush, replacing the rule of the Greeks and Parthians in these regions.

Eventually, the Kushans established their authority over the lower Indus Basin and much of the Gangetic Basin. Their empire extended from the Oxus River to the Ganges River, encompassing Khorasan in Central Asia, parts of Iran, Afghanistan, almost all of Pakistan, and most of northern India. This vast territory under the Kushan rule is sometimes called a Central Asian empire. The empire facilitated significant cultural exchange, leading to the emergence of a unique culture that spanned nine modern countries.

There were two successive dynasties of the Kushans. The first was established by a house of chiefs known as the Kadphises, who ruled for twenty-eight years from around AD 50 under two kings. The first king, Kadphises I, minted copper coins imitating Roman coins in regions south of the Hindu Kush. The second king, Kadphises II, issued many gold coins and expanded his kingdom east of the Indus River. Following the house of Kadphises, the house of Kanishka rose to prominence. Under its kings, Kushan's power extended over upper India and the lower Indus basin. The early Kushan rulers produced numerous gold coins with a higher degree of metallic purity than those from the Gupta Empire. While most of the Kushan gold coins were found west of the Indus, their inscriptions are located not only in northwestern India and Sindh but also in Mathura, Shravasti, Kaushambi, and Varanasi. Thus, they covered much of the middle Gangetic basin besides establishing authority in the Ganga-Yamuna doab.

Kushan coins, inscriptions, constructions, and sculptures discovered in Mathura indicate that it served as their second capital in India, with Purushapura (modern-day Peshawar) being the first. Here, Kanishka built a monastery and a massive stupa, which captivated foreign travelers. Kanishka is the most renowned ruler of the Kushans. Although he faced defeat against the Chinese outside India's borders, he is historically significant for two reasons. First, he established an era in AD 78 known as the Shaka era, which is still used by the Government of India today. Second, Kanishka was a great supporter of Buddhism; he convened a Buddhist council in Kashmir, where the Mahayana form of Buddhism was formalized. In addition to his contributions to religion, Kanishka was a patron of art and architecture.

Shivling Worshipped by The Kushans

Kanishka's successors continued to govern northwestern India until approximately AD 230, and some bore typical Indian names, such as Vasudeva. The

Kushan empire in Afghanistan and the areas west of the Indus was overtaken in the mid-third century by the Sassanian power, which originated in Iran. However, Kushan principalities persisted in India for about another century. The Kushan influence lingered in the Kabul Valley, Kapisa, Bactria, Khorezm, and Sogdiana (present-day Bokhara and Samarkand in Central Asia) during the third to fourth centuries. Many Kushan coins, inscriptions, and terracottas have been discovered in these regions, particularly in Toprak-Kala in Khorezm, south of the Aral Sea on the Oxus River, where a large Kushan palace from the third to fourth centuries has been excavated. This palace housed an administrative archive containing inscriptions and documents written in Aramaic script and the Khorezmian language.

THE INDO-SASSANIANS

However, by the middle of the third century, the Sassanians had occupied the lower Indus region. Initially, they called this region Hindu, not in the sense of religion but in the sense of the Indus people. A Sassanian inscription of AD 262 uses the term Hindustan for this region. Thus, the term Hindustan, which was used for India in Mughal and modern times, was first used in the third century AD. The Sassanians, also called the Indo-Sassanians, ruled India for less than a century but contributed to the Indian economy by issuing many coins.

Though India had shaken off Greco-Macedonian rule just a century and a half earlier, Greece and its vast collection of conquered territories had not forgotten about the Asian subcontinents, a whole of fertile farmland and rich material resources. Accordingly, they delight in its beauty and religious power. At its cultural and territorial height of influence in the years after the breakup of the Mauryan Empire, Greece had expanded into a range of Hellenistic kingdoms and territories—so named because of the word Hellas, meaning Greece. These realms stretched south into North Africa and northward from the Mediterranean into Asia. The Greek territories adjacent to India fell under one of Alexander the Great's generals, Seleucus, and remained in Hellenistic control for several generations.

This proximity produced the Greco-Bactrian and Indo-Greek kingdoms in the far north of the subcontinent. India and its adjacent northern neighbors fell under the heavy influence of the Hellenistic conquerors, while the central part of the subcontinent remained united under the leadership of Emperor Shunga. To the far south, the Kingdom of Kalinga had regained its independence from external empires, as did the Pandyan Dynasty and multiple small to mid-sized regions. Here, a cultural divide began to show between the people of the north and the south. The southern Indians were not untouched by the hands of the Greeks, yet they persevered as a culture of primarily Vedic and Hindu people. In the north, religions were plentiful and even faddish in their adoption, one after another. The northerners, under Asian and Greek rule, practiced Buddhism, Hinduism, Jainism, Hellenism, and Zoroastrianism. Since the Greeks had long worshiped multiple gods, their evolving beliefs merged well with those of their Indian, Chinese, and Pakistani colonies. In eastern central India, Pushyamitra Shunga was a follower of the Vedic god, Lord Shiva, and as such, he put a target on the Buddhists of his realm. Beyond promoting Shiva, Emperor Shunga actively had Buddhists killed to purify his monotheistic beliefs; it is perhaps due to this blatant form of ethnic cleansing that Buddhism shrank so significantly out of favor in most of India. Shunga was just as dedicated to warfare for territorial gain as Ashoka had been against it, and through a series of battles, he took about one-third of the total land India and adjacent regions had to offer. Though Shunga and his nine dynastic successors were quick to the sword, theirs was a period of Indian history in which the arts and education grew. Through royal Shunga patronage, literature, architecture, and the pursuit of higher education and artistic pursuits were achievable for citizens of the empire.

The archaeological record of that period, from about 184 BCE to 73 BCE, includes a variety of finely detailed jewelry, small terra-cotta sculptures, large sculptures, tablets, and architectural monuments. The latter includes the chaitya hall at Bhaja and the renowned Great Stupa at Sanchi. Though the first Emperor Shunga murdered Buddhists outright, later dynastic rulers took a more reverent attitude toward those members of the peaceful faith, repairing the monuments of Ashoka respectfully. Like the early art of the Vedics, Shunga art features many-limbed gods in symbolic dress and pose. It is easy to see how the dominant successor to the Maurya Empire protected much of future India from the changes wrought by Greek cities and kingdoms in the north, primarily in terms of religion.

During this period, Hinduism reigned among the many religious and spiritual paths that characterized that part of the world, so much so that it ceased to be considered a religion as it was a way of living to honor the traditions of one's predecessors. Both the north and south of India were affected economically by the Greek presence in the Middle East, and the whole of the subcontinent used coins struck from a variety of fine metals, including copper and gold. The northern varieties were usually round as per the Greek standard; those in the south retained their classical Indian features and were usually square. The coins featured Hellenistic emperors and Hindu gods, two languages, Greek and Sanskrit. These were used in trade not only within the Greco-Indian kingdoms but also as far away as China.

In approximately 125 BCE, the Greco-Indian constructs were partially conquered by Scythians from eastern regions of Asia. This caused the Greeks to abandon Bactria and move farther south into central India. By the 1st century CE, the Yuezhi tribes of China established the Kushan Empire in what had once been Indo-Greek and Greco-Bactrian strongholds. Once more, the Greeks were removed from the subcontinent—and this time, they would not return.

THE CLASSICAL PERIOD PART 2

THE GUPTA EMPIRE

The Gupta Empire, founded by Chandragupta I around 320 CE (not to be confused with Chandragupta Maurya), is often regarded as a golden age of India. Unlike the Maurya Empire, the Gupta Empire was not highly centralized; it allowed most decisions to be made at the local level. Chandragupta married a Lichchhavi princess from Vaishali and expanded his rule to the far west, as Allahabad, and north to Nepal. However, the empire did not extend farther south than the Ganges River.

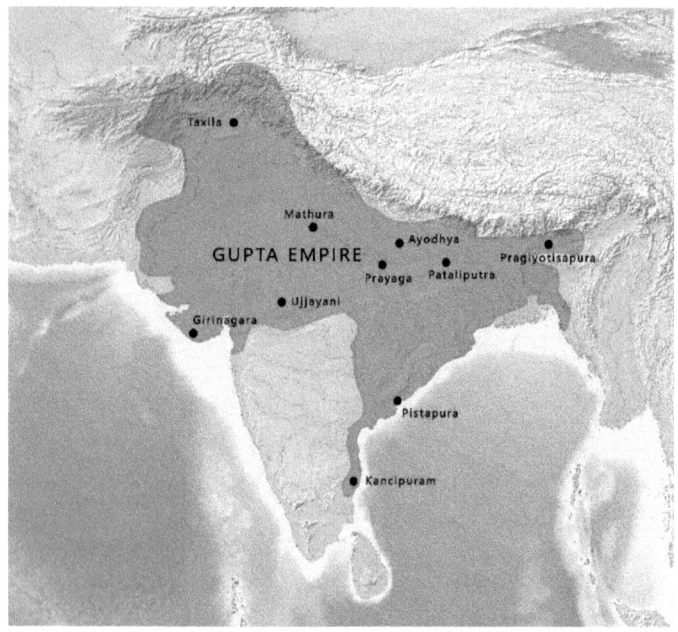

Map of Gupta Empire

His son, Samudragupta, further expanded the empire into the Deccan, reaching as far south as Tamil Nadu, north to Rajasthan and Punjab, and east into Bengal. Many of these territories likely paid him tribute and managed their own affairs, meaning he had financial but not political control over them. This approach proved effective, as the Gupta Empire lasted until 532 CE—more than two centuries.

The Guptas made land grants an essential feature of their rule, restructuring agriculture by providing incentives to convert wasteland into productive land. These grants were offered to individuals and to monasteries, temples, and centers of learning, such as the Buddhist University of Nalanda, which once owned 200 villages. Xuanzang, a Chinese Buddhist monk who visited India from 629 to 645 CE, studied at Nalanda and described it as an earthly paradise, complete with pools filled with blue lotus flowers, vibrant flame trees, and groves of mango trees providing shade. Upon returning to China, he brought back numerous Sanskrit texts, greatly contributing to the expansion of Buddhism in China. Later, in the sixteenth century, novelist Wu Cheng'en adapted his experiences into the classic work "Journey to the West."

Land grants were inscribed on copper plates, and many of these records have survived. This suggests that a bureaucracy and a complex legal structure were in place, where written records played a crucial role. An intriguing aspect of the land grant system is that it allowed small-scale peasant agriculture to coexist with large-scale land ownership and infrastructure projects, such as dams and step-wells (wells with staircases for easy access to groundwater).

During this period, Hinduism evolved, likely partly in response to challenges from the two "reform" religions. The major deities shifted from Agni and Surya, the most important gods of the earlier Vedic period, to Vishnu and Shiva, with shakti, or goddess cults, also emerging. Unlike the Vedic religion, which lacked images of the gods, Hinduism or Sanatana Dharma started representing deities through idols, lingams (phallic symbols), or rocks. Animal sacrifices gradually gave way to puja, which involved offering grains or other vegetables to the deities, and darshan, the viewing of sacred images often concealed behind a gate or curtain that is opened to allow worshippers to see the god.

THE KAMARUPAS

Kamarupa, also called Pragjyotisha-Kamarupa, was an early stage during the classical period on the Indian subcontinent and was the first historical kingdom of Assam. The word Kamrupa first appeared in the Samudragupt edict; before that, there was no mention of its existence.

Copper Plate Seal Kamrupa

Deopahar Head

Though Kamarupa prevailed from 350 to 1140 CE, the Davaka region was absorbed by Kamarupa in the 5th century CE and ruled by three dynasties from their capitals in present-day Guwahati and Tezpur. Kamarupa, at its height, covered the entire Brahmaputra Valley, parts of North Bengal, Bhutan, and the northern part of Bangladesh, and, at times, portions of what is now West Bengal and Bihar. Though the historical kingdom disappeared by the 12th century to be replaced by smaller political entities, the notion of Kamarupa persisted, and ancient and medieval chroniclers continued to call a part of this kingdom Kamrup. In the 16th century, the Ahom Kingdom came into prominence, assumed the legacy of the ancient Kamarupa kingdom, and aspired to extend its kingdom to the Karatoya River.

Kamarupa, an ancient kingdom in the northeastern region of the Indian subcontinent, had several notable achievements:

1. **Cultural and Religious Influence**: Kamarupa was a significant center for the development of Tantric Hinduism. The Kamakhya temple in Guwahati is one of the most important Shakti Peethas and remains a major pilgrimage site.
2. **Architectural Contributions**: The kingdom is known for its unique architectural style, which includes temples like Kamakhya, Umananda, and Navagraha. These structures reflect a blend of indigenous and classical Indian architectural elements.
3. **Literary and Scholarly Works**: Kamarupa was a hub for Sanskrit literature and learning. Scholars from this region contributed to various fields, including astronomy, mathematics, and medicine.
4. **Political Stability and Expansion**: Under the rule of the Varman, Mlechchha, and Pala dynasties, Kamarupa maintained political stability and expanded its territory. It played a crucial role in the regional politics of northeastern India.
5. **Trade and Commerce**: The kingdom had active trade routes connecting it with other parts of India and Southeast Asia. These routes facilitated cultural and economic exchanges, contributing to the region's prosperity.

These achievements highlight Kamarupa's importance in India's historical and cultural landscape.

THE SOUTHERN KINGDOMS

The southernmost region of the Indian Peninsula, located south of the Krishna River, was historically divided into three significant kingdoms: the Chola, the Pandya, and the Chera, also known as Kerala. Among these, the Pandyas hold a prominent place in ancient history; they were first chronicled by the Greek ambassador Megasthenes, who noted their kingdom's famous reputation for exquisite pearls. His accounts also suggest the remarkable presence of matriarchal elements in Pandya society, as he described the kingdom being ruled by a woman.

Geographically, the Pandya territory encompassed the southernmost and southeastern sections of the Indian Peninsula, roughly aligning with today's districts of Tirunelveli, Ramnad, and Madurai in Tamil Nadu, with its majestic capital located in Madurai. The rich cultural tapestry of this region is reflected in the Sangam literature, a compilation of works produced by learned academies in the early centuries of the Christian era. Although this literature does not provide a comprehensive history of the Pandya rulers, it references a few conquerors and vividly depicts a kingdom that was notably wealthy and prosperous.

The Pandyas thrived thanks to robust trade networks with the Roman Empire, even dispatching ambassadors to the Roman Emperor Augustus. The influence of the brahmanas was significant in this society, as the Pandya kings actively participated in Vedic sacrifices, which were a vital aspect of their cultural and religious practices during the early centuries of the Christian era. Thus, the Pandyas were not only a prominent political entity but also a vibrant part of the rich historical landscape of ancient India.

The Chola kingdom, which historically came to be known as Cholamandalam (Coromandel), was situated in early medieval times to the north-east of the Pandyas' territory, strategically located between the Pennar and Velar rivers. Our understanding of the political history of the Cholas largely derives from ancient Sangam literature, which provides insight into their rule and culture. The Cholas had their primary center of political power at Uraiyur, an important city that gained prominence for its thriving cotton trade.

Around the mid-second century BC, a noteworthy Chola king named Elara embarked on his conquest of Sri Lanka, where he established a rule that lasted nearly fifty years. Elara's reign marked a significant chapter in Chola history as it expanded its territory beyond the mainland of southern India. A more comprehensive account of the Chola dynasty begins to emerge in the second century AD, particularly with the reign of the illustrious king Karikala.

King Karikala is celebrated for his remarkable contributions to infrastructure, most notably the founding of the port city of Puhar, which was strategically located on the southeastern coast. He undertook the ambitious project of constructing 160 kilometers of embankments along the Kaveri River, aimed at flood control and irrigation. This extensive construction effort was executed utilizing the labor of approximately 12,000 captives brought from Sri Lanka, highlighting the Chola's capacity for large-scale projects and their reliance on slave labor.

Puhar, which is coterminous with the later known Kaveripattanam, served as the Chola capital and became a central hub for trade and commerce in the region. Archaeological excavations in the area reveal the presence of a significant dock, indicative of the Cholas' robust maritime trade activities. One of the primary sources of wealth for the Chola dynasty was the flourishing trade in cotton textiles, which were highly sought after in international markets. To protect and promote their commercial interests, the Cholas maintained a powerful and efficient navy, which allowed them to engage in trade across the seas.

However, despite the achievements under Karikala and his immediate successors, Chola power began to experience a rapid decline. The capital city of Kaveripattanam eventually fell into ruin, overwhelmed and destroyed by various external pressures. The neighboring powers, primarily the Cheras and the Pandyas, expanded their own territories at the expense of the Cholas. Additionally, aggressive incursions from the Pallavas to the north nearly eradicated what remained of Chola influence by the end of the early medieval period.

From the fourth to the ninth century, the Cholas played a limited role in the broader historical context of southern India, overshadowed by the more dominant Chera and Pandya kingdoms. The Chera kingdom, located to the west and north of the Pandyas, encompassed a narrow strip of land flanked by the Arabian Sea and the Western Ghats, covering significant portions of present-day Kerala and Tamil Nadu.

During the early centuries of the Christian era, the Chera state was as important as its Chola and Pandya counterparts, largely due to its flourishing trade with Roman merchants. The Romans recognized the strategic significance of Muziris, an ancient port city believed to be located at Cranganore within the Chera kingdom, establishing two regiments there to safeguard their trading interests. It is also said that the Romans constructed a temple dedicated to Augustus at this site, highlighting the deep commercial ties between the two civilizations.

The historical narrative of the Cheras is punctuated by continuous conflicts with both the Cholas and the Pandyas. In a notable episode, the Cheras killed the father of King Karikala, although the Chera king also met a tragic fate. Despite this, the two kingdoms experienced periods of uneasy alliances, including a matrimonial alliance that sought to forge peace. At one point, the Chera king aligned himself with the Pandya rulers in their joint efforts against the Cholas. However, the Cholas emerged victorious, and it is recounted that during the battle, the Chera king was grievously wounded in a shameful manner, leading him to take his own life.

The Chera poets provide vivid accounts of their greatest ruler, Senguttuvan, known as the Red or Good Chera. Under his leadership, the Cheras routed their rival factions and successfully established his cousin upon the throne. Legend has it that Senguttuvan undertook an audacious campaign into the northern territories, reportedly crossing the Ganges River—though many historians consider these accounts to be embellished or exaggerated.

Overall, the intricate tapestry of Chola and Chera's history paints a vivid picture of the socio-political dynamics at play in ancient South India, characterized by ambition, rivalry, and shifting alliances that shaped the region's historical trajectory.

After the second century, the power of the Chera dynasty declined, and we have little information about its history until the eighth century. The political history of the three main kingdoms is primarily characterized by the ongoing wars they waged against each other and against Sri Lanka. Although these conflicts weakened the states, they benefited significantly from their natural resources and foreign trade.

These kingdoms cultivated various spices, especially pepper, which was highly sought after in the Western world. They also had elephants that supplied valuable ivory. The seas offered pearls, and the mines produced precious stones, both of which were exported to the West in large quantities. Additionally, they were known for producing muslin and silk. Early Tamil poems even describe cotton cloth as thin as a snake's slough, and Uraiyur was recognized for its cotton trade.

In ancient times, the Tamils engaged in trade with the Hellenistic kingdoms of Egypt and Arabia on one side, and with the Malay Archipelago and China on the other. This extensive trading network led to several Greek words for rice, ginger, cinnamon, and other goods being derived from Tamil. When Egypt became a Roman province and the monsoon season was discovered around the beginning of the first century AD, this trade received a significant boost. Thus, the southern kingdoms engaged in a profitable trade with the Romans for the first two and a half centuries. However, as this trade began to decline, the kingdoms subsequently started to decay.

VARDHAN DYNASTY

Lion Statue of Stone 7th Century

The **Pushyabhuti dynasty**, also known as the **Vardhana dynasty**, was the ruling dynasty of the Kingdom of Thanesar and later the Kingdom of Kannauj in northern India during the 6th and 7th centuries. The dynasty reached its zenith under its last ruler, Harshvardhana (c. 590 – c. 647 CE). Its empire covered much of north and north-western India, extending to Kamrupa in the east and the Narmada River in the south. The dynasty initially ruled from Sthanveshvara (modern-day Thanesar, Haryana), but Harsha eventually made Kanyakubja (modern-day Kannauj, Uttar Pradesh) his capital, from where he ruled until 647 CE.

The Guptas, who held power in Uttar Pradesh and Bihar, ruled over northern and western India for approximately 160 years until the mid-sixth century. After their decline, northern India fragmented into several kingdoms. Around AD 500, the white Hunas asserted their dominance over Kashmir, Punjab, and western India. During this period, control of northern and western India fell to about half a dozen feudatories who divided the Gupta Empire among themselves.

Gradually, one of these dynasties gained control over Thanesar in Haryana and extended its influence over the other feudatories. This unification was brought about by Harshavardhana (AD 606–647). Excavations at 'Harsha ka Tila' in Thanesar have revealed some brick structures, but they cannot be definitively identified as parts of a palace. Harsha established Kanauj as his seat of power, from where he expanded his authority in all directions.

By the seventh century, Pataliputra, once a thriving hub of power and commerce, encountered significant challenges that led to its decline. The decline can be traced to several interconnected factors. Pataliputra's strength and relevance in the ancient Indian political landscape were largely attributed to its strategic position as a center of trade and commerce. Merchants from diverse regions—east, west, north, and south—flocked to the city, navigating through its waters via four major rivers that facilitated trade. This bustling economic activity allowed for the collection of tolls, which not only enriched the city's coffers but also played a crucial role in sustaining its infrastructure and maintaining the salaries of government officials and military personnel.

However, as trade routes fell into disrepair and economic activity slowed, the vibrant marketplace that once characterized Pataliputra began to fade. The scarcity of money became increasingly evident; officers and soldiers who had been accustomed to regular pay now had to rely on land grants as their primary source of income. This shift in the economic structure weakened the city's influence and stability, as it became increasingly challenging to maintain a well-functioning government and a capable military presence.

In the vacuum left by Pataliputra's decline, power began to gravitate toward military camps known as skandhavaras and strategically located regions that could exert control over vast expanses of land. One such area was Kanauj, situated in the Farrukhabad district of Uttar Pradesh. This region began to rise in prominence around the second half of the sixth century. Under the reign of Harsha, Kanauj emerged as a significant political power, marking the advent of the feudal age in northern India. In stark contrast to Pataliputra, which represented a pre-feudal order characterized by centralized authority and trade-based wealth, Kanauj's rise signified a shift towards localized control and military fortification.

Geographically, Kanauj possessed natural advantages that further facilitated its ascendancy. Its elevated terrain made it an ideal location for fortification, challenging for invaders to breach. Positioned at the heart of the doab—the region between the Ganges and Yamuna rivers—Kanauj was not only defensively advantageous but also strategically located for military maneuvers. By the seventh century, it had become a well-fortified bastion, allowing rulers to project power and control across the eastern and western sections of the doab. This accessibility enabled the swift movement of troops via both land and water routes, enhancing Kanauj's prowess as a center of military and political authority in the region.

The early history of Harsha's reign is reconstructed through the writings of Banabhatta, his court poet, who authored the book "Harshacharita." This information is further supplemented by the account of the Chinese pilgrim Hsuan Tsang, who visited India in the seventh century and stayed for about fifteen years. Harsha's inscriptions provide insights into various types of taxes and officials during his rule. While Harsha is regarded as the last great Hindu emperor of India, he was neither a strict Hindu nor the ruler of the entire country. His authority was primarily limited to northern India, excluding Kashmir. He had direct control over regions such as Rajasthan, Punjab, Uttar Pradesh, Bihar, and Orissa, although his influence extended over a much larger area. It seems that many peripheral states acknowledged his sovereignty. In eastern India, he faced resistance from the Shaivite king Shashanka of Gauda, who notably destroyed the Bodhi tree at Bodh-Gaya. However, Shashanka's death in AD 619 brought an end to this conflict.

Harsha's southward expansion was halted at the Narmada River by the Chalukya king Pulakeshin, who governed a significant portion of what is now Karnataka and Maharashtra, with his capital at Badami in the

Bijapur district of Karnataka. Other than this setback, Harsha faced little serious opposition and succeeded in establishing a measure of political unity across much of India.

Harshavardhana's reign exemplifies the transition from ancient to medieval times. He governed his empire similarly to the Guptas; however, his administration had become more feudal and decentralized. It is reported that Harsha maintained an army of 100,000 horses and 60,000 elephants, which is remarkable considering that the Mauryas, who ruled over nearly the entire subcontinent except for the deep south, had only 30,000 cavalry and 9,000 elephants. Harsha's larger army could be attributed to his ability to mobilize support from his feudatories in times of war. Each feudatory contributed a quota of foot soldiers and horses, significantly enhancing the imperial army. The vast numbers in Harsha's military suggest a substantial increase in the population.

Land grants continued to be issued to priests for special services rendered to the state. More notably, Harsha is credited with granting land to officials through the issuance of charters. These grants provided the same concessions to priests as those given in earlier periods. The Chinese pilgrim Hsuan Tsang informs us that Harsha's revenues were divided into four parts: one part for the king's expenses, a second for scholars, a third for endowing officials and public servants, and a fourth for religious purposes. He also noted that ministers and high-ranking state officers were given land grants. This feudal practice of rewarding officers with land appears to have originated under Harsha, which may explain the scarcity of coins issued during his reign.

In Harsha's empire, law and order were not effectively maintained. Hsuan Tsang, who likely received special care from the government, reported being robbed, even though he noted that severe punishments were prescribed for crimes. Robbery was considered a form of treason, punishable by the amputation of the robber's right hand. However, it seems that under the influence of Buddhism, the harshness of these punishments was reduced, and some criminals were sentenced to life imprisonment instead.

The reign of Harsha is historically significant due to the visit of the Chinese pilgrim Hsuan Tsang, who left China in AD 629 and traveled all the way to India. After a lengthy stay in India, he returned to China in AD 645. He came to study at the Buddhist University of Nalanda, located in the district of the same name in Bihar, and to collect Buddhist texts. Hsuan Tsang spent many years in Harsha's court and traveled extensively throughout India. Influenced by him, Harsha became a great supporter of Buddhism and made generous endowments to the religion.

Hsuan Tsang vividly describes court life during Harsha's reign, providing a richer and more reliable account than that of Fa-Hsien. His observations shed light on the social and economic conditions and the religious sects of the period. The Chinese pilgrim noted that Pataliputra and Vaishali were in a state of decline, while Prayag and Kanauj in the Doab region had become more prominent.

The accounts indicate that the Brahmanas and Kshatriyas led simple lives, while the nobles and priests lived in luxury. This highlights a distinction between the ranks of the two higher varnas. Most individuals within these varnas likely engaged in agriculture. Hsuan Tsang referred to the Shudras as agriculturists, which is significant because earlier texts depicted them as serving the three higher varnas.

Additionally, Hsuan Tsang observed the living conditions of untouchable communities, such as scavengers and executioners, who resided outside the villages. These individuals consumed garlic and onions, and upon entering a town, they would announce their arrival loudly to ensure that people kept their distance.

Harsha adopted a tolerant religious policy. Initially a Shaiva, he gradually became a significant patron of Buddhism. As a devout Buddhist, he convened a grand assembly at Kanauj to promote the doctrines of Mahayana Buddhism. This assembly was attended by notable figures, including Hsuan Tsang, the ruler of Kamarupa, Bhaskaravarman, as well as kings from twenty different states and several thousand priests from various sects.

To accommodate the attendees, two thatched halls were built, each capable of holding 1,000 people. However, the centerpiece of the assembly was a massive tower that housed a golden statue of the Buddha, which was as tall as Harsha himself. He worshipped this image and hosted a public dinner.

The conference was initiated by Hsuan Tsang, who elaborated on the virtues of Mahayana Buddhism and challenged the audience to refute his arguments. For five days, no one responded. Eventually, some of his theological rivals conspired to take Hsuan Tsang's life. Upon learning of this plot, Harsha threatened to behead anyone who harmed him.

Suddenly, the great tower caught fire and there was an attempt on Harsha's life. In response, he arrested 500 Brahmanas, banished most of them, and executed a few. This series of events suggests that Harsha may not have been as tolerant as he is often portrayed.

Following his triumph at Kanauj, King Harsha convened a grand assembly at Prayag, a gathering that drew the attention of tributary princes, ministers, nobles, and various dignitaries from across his realm. This significant event included the worship of an exquisite image of Buddha, while the renowned Buddhist monk Hsuan Tsang captivated the audience with his enlightening discourses. At the culmination of the assembly, Harsha demonstrated his generosity by making substantial donations, so lavish that, according to tradition, he reportedly distributed everything he owned except for the clothes on his back.

Hsuan Tsang, who traveled through Harsha's expansive empire, sang the praises of the king, portraying him as gracious, kind-hearted, and exceedingly supportive. The pilgrim was allowed to explore the diverse regions of Harsha's realm, deeply appreciating the cultural richness he encountered. In addition, Banabhatta, a well-known poet, delivered an ornate and flattering narrative of Harsha's early reign in his literary work, "Harshacharita". This work showcased

Banabhatta's skill and established a stylistic precedent for future writers.

Harsha is celebrated not just for his royal patronage and commitment to learning but also for his association with the composition of three notable plays: "Priyadarshika", "Ratnavali", and "Nagananda". Banabhatta, a Sanskrit poet in the court of Harsha Vardhan, in his writings, highlights Harsha's poetic talents, suggesting that he was a monarch of considerable literary merit. However, this claim is met with skepticism by several medieval scholars, who argue that these dramas were, in fact, penned by an individual named Dhavaka, who attributed them to Harsha for personal gain. While it is possible that Harsha may have contributed some literary pieces, a prevailing proverb suggests that royal authorship often lacks authenticity.

In both ancient and medieval India, kings were often lauded for a wide range of accomplishments, one of the most notable being their literary prowess. This practice of glorifying a monarch's support for the arts and literature served as a strategic method to enhance their royal image and solidify their authority. The tradition can be traced back to Harishena, who initiated this custom during the reign of the illustrious Samudragupta, a ruler of the Gupta Empire known for his military conquests and cultural patronage.

Under Harsha's reign, the practice of magnifying kings' achievements became even more pronounced and deeply entrenched in India's political and cultural landscape. Harsha patronized poets and playwrights, and his court became a vibrant center for literary and artistic expression. This tradition not only aimed to gain favor from the king by acknowledging his contributions to culture but also served to elevate his status and legitimize his rule in the eyes of his subjects and the surrounding rivals.

The deliberate fostering of a king's literary and cultural contributions helped create a narrative depicting the monarch as a wise and enlightened leader. It acted as a means for the king to assert his superiority over competitors and to unify his subjects under a shared cultural identity, reinforcing his power and influence across the realm. Through this intricate interplay of patronage and propaganda, the legacy of kings was carefully crafted, highlighting their pivotal role in the development of literature, art, and culture in ancient and medieval Indian society.

CHAPTER 11
SANGAM LITERATURE

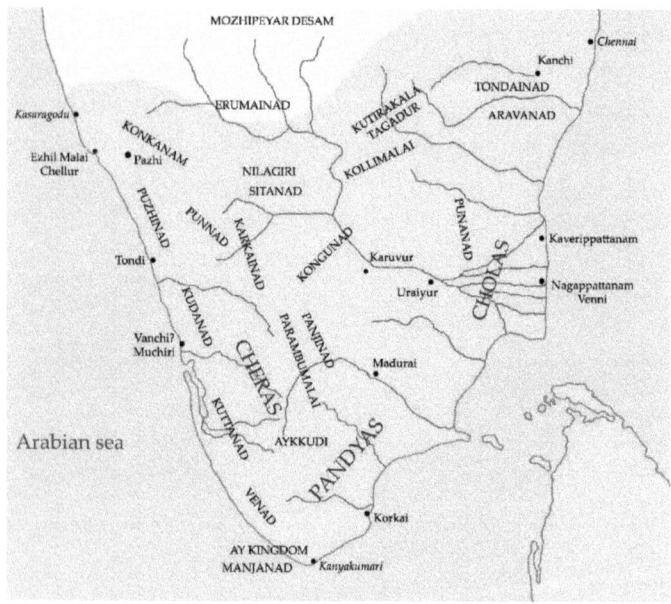

South India in Sangam Period

The insights regarding the life of the Tamils during the early historical period predominantly draw from the rich corpus of Sangam literature. This literature emerged from a renowned assembly, the Sangam, a poetic college or a gathering of Tamil poets. It is widely believed that the Sangam functioned under the patronage of various local chiefs or kings, providing a supportive environment for artistic and literary expression.

However, the specifics regarding the number of Sangam sessions and the exact timeline over which they were convened remain primarily ambiguous.

A Tamil commentary from the middle of the eighth century asserts that three distinct Sangams collectively spanned an astonishing 9990 years, attracting an impressive cohort of 8598 poets and enjoying the sponsorship of 197 Pandya kings. Such figures are likely to be exaggerated, reflecting more of a mythological or symbolic nature rather than being strictly historical. What is more reliably acknowledged is that at least one Sangam took place in Madurai, a city that holds a significant place in Tamil history and culture.

The Sangam literature, which was crafted during these gatherings, was ultimately compiled between AD 300 and 600. Interestingly, sections of this literary heritage reference earlier periods, with certain works tracing back to at least the second century AD. The Sangam literature can be broadly categorized into two primary types: narrative and didactic.

The narrative component, called Melkannakku or the Eighteen Major Works, consists of eighteen key texts, encompassing eight anthologies and ten idylls. These works are rich in storytelling and depict various aspects of life, love, courage, and nature in ancient Tamil society. On the other hand, the didactic literature, termed Kilkanakku or the Eighteen Minor Works, focuses more on moral teachings, philosophical implications, and practical knowledge, providing insights into the values and ethics of the time.

In summary, while the details surrounding the Sangam and its literature may be shrouded in ambiguity and exaggeration, its significance in Tamil history and culture remains profound and lasting. The Sangam literature reflects the societal norms and artistic expressions of the period and serves as a crucial link to understanding the Tamil identity through the ages.

The various forms of narrative texts from ancient Tamil literature reveal a complex progression of social evolution among the early Tamil people. These texts are recognized as significant works of heroic poetry that celebrate the courage and exploits of legendary figures, thus glorifying what can be deemed a heroic age. Central to these narratives are frequent references to ongoing conflicts, including perpetual wars and cattle raids, which indicate a society deeply entrenched in a culture of warfare and competition.

Early Tamil society was portrayed as predominantly pastoral, with people living close to their herds and flocks. Interestingly, the Sangam texts provide valuable insights into the megalithic period that preceded this heroic age. The early megalithic inhabitants seem to have been a diverse group comprised mainly of pastoralists, hunters, and fishermen, alongside evidence suggesting they also practiced agriculture, notably rice cultivation.

Archaeological findings across numerous sites in peninsular India reveal an array of agricultural tools, such as hoes and sickles, instrumental for farming; however, the absence of plowshares suggests a different mode of agrarian practice, likely reflective of a less settled lifestyle. In addition to these farming implements, a rich assortment of iron tools has been unearthed. These include wedges, flat celts, arrowheads, long swords, lances, spikes, and spearheads. Such tools appear to have been predominantly designed for purposes related to warfare and hunting, echoing the themes expressed in the Sangam texts, which convey a society perpetually on the brink of conflict over resources and territory.

The narratives indicate that the acquisition of war booty played a vital role in the sustenance and livelihood of these early communities, highlighting the significance of warfare as a means of economic support. Furthermore, a poignant theme emerges around the concept of mortality and legacy within these texts; they state that when a hero meets his end, he is metaphorically reduced to a mere piece of stone. This imagery resonates strongly with the burial practices of the megalithic people, known for their construction of large stone circles over graves, a ritual that seems to have evolved into the later custom of erecting hero stones, or virarkal. These stones were raised to honor the memory of valiant heroes who sacrificed their lives for their kin and their communities.

Thus, it becomes apparent that the earliest layers of social evolution reflected in the Sangam works are closely intertwined with the cultural practices and social structures of early megalithic society. They offer a glimpse into a dynamic past characterized by conflict, honor, and a profound reverence for those who fought bravely in the name of survival and legacy.

The Sangam texts, a rich collection of literature from ancient Tamil Nadu, offer valuable insights into the early stages of state formation in this region. These narratives describe a society where armies were composed of brave groups of warriors, laying the groundwork for a taxation system and a rudimentary judicial framework. The texts illuminate the vibrant tapestry of trade, showcasing merchants bustling about, skilled craftsmen creating their wares, and diligent farmers tending to their fields. Notable towns such as Kanchi, Korkai, Madurai, Puhar, and Uraiyur emerge from these writings, with Puhar, also known as Kaveripattanam, standing out as the most significant hub of activity.

The references made in the Sangam texts regarding towns and economic practices are further supported by ancient Greek and Roman accounts, alongside archaeological findings from various Sangam sites. Many of these texts, including the didactic ones, were composed by Brahmana scholars proficient in Prakrit and Sanskrit. The didactic literature, dating back to the early centuries of the Christian era, establishes a code of conduct not just for kings and their courts but also for the diverse social strata and occupations within the society—a distinction that emerged prominently after the fourth century due to a rise in the number of Brahmanas under the patronage of the Pallavas.

Additionally, Sangam literature alludes to generous village grants and describes the royal lineage through the notable solar and lunar dynasties, each with its storied heritage. Among these prominent texts is the Tolkkappiyam, which explores the intricacies of grammar and poetics. Another invaluable Tamil work is the Tirukkural, a philosophical text brimming with wise maxims.

Two remarkable Tamil epics, Silappadikaram and Manimekalai, were composed around the sixth century. Silappadikaram, often hailed as the crowning jewel of early Tamil literature, intricately weaves a poignant love story involving a nobleman named Kovalan, who finds himself enamored with a courtesan named Madhavi from Kaveripattanam, much to the chagrin of his devoted wife, Kannagi. The author of this epic is believed to be a Jaina storyteller, who artfully sets the narrative against the backdrop of various kingdoms within Tamilakam.

Conversely, Manimekalai, authored by a grain merchant from Madurai, narrates the adventurous journey of Kovalan and Madhavi's daughter. While it holds greater significance from a religious perspective than purely literary, both epics claim connections to the Chera king Senguttuvan, who reigned during the second century AD. Although their exact dating is debated, these epics shed light on Tamil life's social and economic fabric up until approximately the sixth century.

The Tamils mastered the art of writing well before the dawn of the Christian era. Evidence of this can be found in twelve locations across the south, where Ashokan inscriptions in Brahmi script have been discovered—three in Andhra and nine in Karnataka. In the Madurai region alone, over seventy-five short inscriptions dating approximately two centuries later have been unearthed in natural caves, showcasing the oldest forms of Tamil interspersed with Prakrit vocabulary. These inscriptions, dating back to the second-first century BC, were likely made during the influx of Jaina and Buddhist missionaries to the area. Pottery shards, too, have been uncovered during recent archaeological excavations, providing examples of the Tamil language at the onset of the Christian era.

The establishment of writing practices allowed for the flourishing of Sangam literature, which was produced throughout the early centuries of the Christian era and gradually compiled by AD 600, leaving an indelible mark on the literary landscape of Tamil Nadu.

www.ingramcontent.com/pod-product-compliance
Lightning Source LLC
LaVergne TN
LVHW061342080526
838199LV00093B/6900